Praise for

"Readable book. . . . Provocative . . . recommended for psychology and mental health collections, where it may be useful for self-help and encouragement. . . . [A] guide to halting this insidious form of mental abuse and neglect."

—*Library Journal*

"McBride presents specific steps toward recovery that daughters of any age can use as they grieve for the love and support they didn't receive. . . . The author provides parenting tips as well as advice for maintaining healthy love relationships and friendships. . . . An excellent bibliography rounds out this revealing book, which ends on a hopeful and pragmatic note."

—*Publishers Weekly* (starred review)

"*Will I Ever Be Good Enough?* illuminates a very common and unnamed wound—the wound that results from growing up with a narcissistic mother. In this engaging book, Karyl McBride provides a clear, honest, and effective way to heal this wound and live life fully and joyfully."

—Christiane Northrup, M.D., author of *Mother-Daughter Wisdom, The Wisdom of Menopause,* and *Women's Bodies, Women's Wisdom*

"Narcissistic mothers are always there when they need you. They expect to be the center of attention, and they can be cruel if they don't get what they want. Learning how to set boundaries with narcissistic mothers is a complex challenge. Dr. McBride offers a step-by-step approach to understanding narcissism, setting limits on the abuse, and recovering from the psychological damage. This book is a 'must-read' for every woman living in the shadow of a domineering, self-focused parent."

—Nanette Gartrell, M.D., author of *My Answer Is NO . . . If That's Okay with You: How Women Can Say NO and (Still) Feel Good About It*

"The long-term destructive consequences that narcissistic parents have for their children are well known. Until now, however, there has been little in the way of helpful advice for those who were raised by these parents. In this insightful new book, Dr. McBride presents a detailed examination of narcissistic mothers and the harmful effects on their daughters. She also offers practical, step-by-step guidance for working through these issues. This book is a terrific resource for those women raised by narcissistic mothers and looking for strategies for change."
— W. Keith Campbell, Ph.D., author of *When You Love a Man Who Loves Himself*

"*Will I Ever Be Good Enough?* is an amazing journey out of pain. Providing true professional guidance and clarity, Dr. Karyl McBride heaps in genuine love and kindness. This book is like having an ideal therapist at your convenience who really helps you heal self-doubt and self-rejection. Every page is milk and honey to your soul."
— Tama J. Kieves, author of *This Time I Dance! Trusting the Journey of Creating the Work You Love (How One Harvard Lawyer Left It All to Have It All!)*

"Excellent clinical information about the effects of narcissistic mothers on their daughters, written clearly for all women struggling with this issue. The recovery section offers a rich variety of ideas and techniques to use in everyday life."
— Linda Vaughan, M.A., Licensed Professional Counselor

"Dr. McBride has broken new and exceptionally important ground in exploring a critical area in parenting. This book is must reading for both the professional and the layperson who want to understand and successfully address the lifelong and potentially devastating impact of narcissistic maternal child rearing. It is filled with useful information and recommendations presented in a readable form."
— David N. Bolocofsky, J.D., Ph.D., family law attorney and former psychology professor

"Dr. McBride does a beautiful job of describing the many faces of narcissism. I found this book extremely engaging and easy to read, and yet it is also highly informative, practical, and structured in its treatment approach. This is a must-read for anyone dealing with a loved one who is narcissistic."
—Renee Richker, M.D., child and adolescent psychiatrist

"[C]omes across with such richness and authenticity that this book should be on every family therapist's shelf. It is written for the daughters, not for clinicians per se; however, both the daughters and their mental health professionals can benefit from the information presented in this volume. . . . Practical, insightful, and full of compassion, it is likely to help many women in ways that few other resources are able to do. [D]aughters of mothers with borderline, antisocial, and histrionic traits are likely to benefit from its caring, empathy, and practicality just as much as daughters of narcissistic mothers. . . . [T]his book is a gem . . . it truly helps the reader to reflect on her pain, as well as relish the hope that she can end the legacy of narcissism."
—Farrah M. Hughes, Ph.D., for *The Family Psychologist,*
newsletter of the Society for Family Psychology, division
43 of the American Psychological Association

WILL I EVER
BE GOOD ENOUGH?

HEALING THE DAUGHTERS OF
NARCISSISTIC MOTHERS

KARYL McBRIDE, PH.D.

FREE PRESS

New York   London   Toronto   Sydney

FREE PRESS
A Division of Simon & Schuster, Inc.
1230 Avenue of the Americas
New York, NY 10020

First Free Press trade paperback edition September 2009

FREE PRESS and colophon are trademarks of Simon & Schuster, Inc.

For information about special discounts for bulk purchases,
please contact Simon & Schuster Special Sales at 1-866-506-1949 or
business@simonandschuster.com

The Simon & Schuster Speakers Bureau can bring authors to
your live event. For more information or to book an event
contact the Simon & Schuster Speakers Bureau at 1-866-248-3049
or visit our website at www.simonspeakers.com

Book design by Julie Schroeder

Manufactured in the United States of America

20 19 18 17 16 15 14 13 12

The Library of Congress has cataloged the hardcover edition as follows:
McBride, Karyl.
    Will I ever be good enough? Healing the daughters of narcissistic
mothers/Karyl McBride.
        p.   cm.
    Includes bibliographical references and index.
    1. Narcissism. 2. Self-acceptance. 3. Mothers and daughters—
Psychology. I. McBride, Karyl. II. Title.
RC553.N36W54 2008
616.85'854—dc22   2008014676

ISBN 978-1-4165-5132-4
ISBN 978-1-4391-2943-2 (pbk)
ISBN 978-1-4391-2323-2 (ebook)

AUTHOR'S NOTE

The examples, anecdotes, and characters in this book are drawn from my clinical work, research, and life experience with real people and events. Names and some identifying features and details have been changed, and in some instances people or situations are composites.

Dedicated to five people who
taught me the essence of unconditional love:

Nathan Scott
Meggan Marie
McKenzie Irene
Isabella Grace
Flora Teresa

ACKNOWLEDGMENTS

For me, writing a book meant slamming into brick walls, climbing them, facing them again, climbing them yet again—an Olympic-size mental workout. It has been stressful, but most importantly, a meaningful labor of love, and certainly a task one does not master in isolation. While a thank-you seems hardly enough, I want to express my heartfelt gratitude to the special people who accompanied me on this trek of passion.

First and foremost, my children and grandchildren: Nate and Paula, Meg and Dave, McKenzie, Isabella, Ken and Al. The love, patience, understanding, and encouragement of family can never be valued highly enough. I love you all so very much.

My agent, Susan Schulman: Your belief in me and this topic repeatedly amazed me. Your professionalism, kindness, hard work, and support will never be forgotten.

Leslie Meredith, senior editor at Free Press: A special gratitude for your keen editorial assistance, your acuity in understanding the sensitive material, and your sincere belief in the need for this book.

Donna Loffredo, editorial assistant at Free Press: Thank you, Donna, for your kind patience with my never-ending questions. I could always hear your warm smile over the phone lines!

Thanks to the staff at Free Press for the final phases

of "spit and polish"! Jeanette Gingold and Edith Lewis, your copyediting work on the manuscript was not only detailed and brilliant, but so very respectful.

Beth Lieberman: Your editing expertise and ability to hang in there caused many days of gratitude. Thank you so much for everything.

Other professionals who assisted with initial editing, proposal work, ideas, and support: Schatzie, Dr. Doreen Orion, Colleen Hubbard, Liz Netzel, Jan Snyder, and Laura Bellotti. A special thanks to you all.

Professional colleagues who took time out of their busy schedules to be readers: Dr. Renee Richker, Dr. David Bolocofsky, and Linda Vaughan. How kind of each of you to offer your time and support, when I know you are all so busy. I am more than grateful for your professional input!

Dr. Jim Gregory, thank you so much for the health section consultation. Your time and kindness are greatly appreciated.

Chris Passerella, the Web site guru with Kitzmiller Design, you were and are so awesome. Thank you for all your time, technical work, and support.

Chris Segura, with Chris' Computer Consulting, Inc., your computer assistance was always timely and helpful. Thanks for the formatting guidance at the eleventh hour. Your patience with my lack of computer sense was a gift.

A special thanks to the people who helped keep me organized and fixed those things that were falling down around me: Gretchen Byron, Carolina Dilullo, Helen Laxson, Marv Endes, Frank Martin, Linda Fangman, and Jessica Dennis.

Tama Kieves and Peg Blackmore: my inspiration and professional support system. You both rock with maternal kindness and blanket understanding.

My dear friends who gave support with love, smiles, hugs, and encouragement: Kay Brandt, Kate Heit, Jim Gronewold, Jim Vonderohe, the Saccomanno crew: Franklin (neighborhood smiles at dawn), Frank (from curmudgeons to Pollyannas and round and round), Gianna (superhero), and Anthony (you rock). E-hugs and thanks to my fifth-grade pal Jimmy Hirsch.

A special thank-you to Ethel Kloos-Fenn from Applied Research Consultants for initial research assistance. I love you and miss you, Ethel.

Thanks to my parents for teaching me about perseverance, good work ethic, and fighting for what you believe in. "Get back on the horse" had an impact!

And finally, a deeply felt thank-you is expressed to the remarkable clients and interviewees who gave time and emotional energy to share personal stories so that other people could be helped. I cannot name you, but you know who you are. This book could not have been written without you and your spirited, daring sense of courage.

CONTENTS

CONTENTS

INTRODUCTION

Our relationship with Mother is birthed simultaneously with our entry into the world. We take our first breath of life, and display the initial dependent, human longing for protection and love in her presence. We are as one in the womb and on the birthing table. This woman, our mother . . . all that she is and is not . . . has given us life. Our connection with her in this instant and from this point forward carries with it tremendous psychological weight for our lifelong well-being. Oddly, I have never wanted to believe this.

First, being a feminist-era mom myself, I didn't want mothers and women to bear so much responsibility or ultimate blame if things go wrong. Certainly many factors other than mothering shape a child's life. Second, I didn't want to face how feeling like an unmothered child had such a devastating effect on me and my life. To acknowledge this meant I had to face it.

While doing research over the years, I have read many books that discuss the mother-daughter bond. Each time I read a different volume, unexpected tears would stream down my cheeks. For I could not recall attachment, closeness, memories of the scent of Mother's perfume, the feel of her skin, the sound of her voice singing in the kitchen, the solace of her rocking, holding and comforting, the intellectual stimulation and joy of being read to.

I knew this was not natural, but could not find a book that explained this lack. It made me feel somewhat crazy. Was I delusional, or just a chick with a poor memory? I could not find a book that explained that this phenomenon of feeling unmothered could be a real deal and that there could be mothers who are not maternal. Nor could I find a book that discussed the conflicted feelings that their daughters have about these mothers, the frustrated love, and even sometimes the hatred. Because good girls aren't supposed to hate their mothers, they don't talk about these bad feelings. Motherhood is a sacred institution in most cultures and therefore is generally not discussed in a negative light. When I decided to write a book on mothers who don't mother their daughters, and the pain this causes girls and adult daughters, I felt as if I were breaking a taboo.

Reading books about the mother-daughter bond always gave me the sensation of a deep loss and the fear that I was alone in this suffering. Experts wrote of the complexity of the mother-daughter connection, how it is rife with conflict and ambivalence, but I felt something different—a void, a lack of empathy and interest, and a lack of feeling loved. For many years, I did not understand and tried to rationalize it. Other members of the family and well-intentioned therapists explained it away with various excuses. Like a good girl, I tried to make excuses and take all the blame. It was not until I began to understand that the emotional void was a characteristic result of maternal narcissism that the pieces began to fit together. The more I learned about maternal narcissism, the more my experience, my sadness, and my lack of memory made sense. This understanding was the key to my beginning to recover my own sense of identity, apart from my mother. I became more centered, taking up what I now call substantial space, no longer invisible (even to myself) and not having to make myself up as I go along. Without understanding, we flail around, we make mistakes, feel deep unworthiness, and sabotage ourselves and our lives.

Writing this book has been a culmination of years of research and a soul journey that took me back to when I was a little girl who knew something was wrong, feeling that the absence of nurturing was not normal, but not knowing why. I am writing this book now in the hopes that I can help other women understand that those feelings were and are not their fault.

This does not mean that I want you to blame your mother. This is not a journey of projected anger, resentment, or rage, but one of understanding. We want to heal ourselves and we have to do that with love and forgiveness for ourselves and our mothers. I do not believe in creating victims. We are accountable for our own lives and feelings. To be healthy, we first have to understand what we experienced as daughters of narcissistic mothers, and then we can move forward in recovery to make things the way they need to be for us. Without understanding our mothers and what their narcissism did to us, it is impossible to recover. We have been taught to repress and deny, but we have to face the truth of our experiences—that our longing for a maternal warmth and mothering is not going to be fulfilled and our wishing and hoping that things will be different are not going to change things. As girls, we were programmed to look at the dynamics of the family in a positive light, even though we knew we lived under a shadow. Our families usually did look good to outsiders, but though we sensed something was wrong, we were told that really "it is nothing." This kind of emotional environment and dishonesty can be crazy-making. Smile, be pretty, and act like everything's good. Sound familiar?

I am still amazed whenever I talk to other daughters of narcissistic mothers at the similarities of our internal emotional landscapes. We may have different lifestyles and outward appearances for the world to see, but inside, we wave the same emotional banners. My greatest hope is that this book will offer you acknowledgment and validation for your profound emotions and allow you to feel whole, healthy, and authentic in who you are today.

In writing this book, I had to fight many internal battles. First, I had to trust my ability to do it, as I am a therapist, not a writer. Second, and of more interest, I had to talk to my mother about it. When I brought it up with Mother, I said to her, "Hey, Mom, I need your help. I am writing a book about mothers and daughters and I need your input, suggestions, and permission to use some personal material." My mother, bless her heart, said, "Why don't you write a book about fathers?" And of course, she was worried about being a bad

mother, which would be expected. She was able to give me her blessing, however, and I think it is because she was trying to understand
that this is not a book about blame, but a book about healing. I have
to admit I wanted her to say many things like: "Are there some things
we need to discuss or work on together?" "Do you have pain from
your childhood?" "Is there anything we can do about it now?" "Can
we heal together?" None of this happened, but after all these years of
my own recovery work, I knew not to expect her to be able to do this
empathic inquiry. I was grateful that I had mustered the nerve to
broach the book to her, which admittedly took me some time to do.
At one time in my life, this exchange would have been unthinkable.

Somehow, after taking this risk, I found it easier to move forward
and be authentic in talking about my own experience as well as about
my research. Although it would have felt emotionally safe to write at
arm's length from a purely clinical perspective, I hope that my own
stories of being a daughter of a narcissistic mother will help you know
that I do understand. I have been there.

I've divided the book into three parts that parallel my approach
to psychotherapy. Part 1 explains the problem of maternal narcissism.
Part 2 shows the impact of the problem, its many effects, and how it
plays out in daughters' lifestyles. Part 3 is a road map for recovery.

I invite you now to come with me to learn about yourself and
your mother. It won't always be a comfortable and easy trip. You'll
be emerging from denial, confronting difficult feelings, being vulnerable, and facing characteristics of your own that you may not like. It
is an emotional undertaking. Sometimes you will find it funny. Other
times you will feel a great sadness as you try to understand what you
experienced and heal from it. By doing so, you will change the legacy
of distorted maternal love and make a lasting difference for your
daughters, sons, and grandchildren. As you face the honest reflections
of your life patterns, you will ultimately like yourself more and become better at parenting, in relationships, and in everything else in
your life.

Emotional legacies are like genetic legacies; they pass along to each generation without anyone really taking a lot of notice. Some of the "hand me downs" are endearing and wonderful and we feel grateful and proud, but some are heartbreaking and destructive. They need to be stopped. We need to stop them. Having done my own recovery work from my distorted maternal legacy, I can say that I've been there and I can help you change yours too.

I welcome you to read further with me. Sit with me, talk with me, cry with me, laugh with me. Together we will begin to deal with the reality of your emotional legacy. Even if it's always been "all about Mom," it's your turn now. It gets to be about you, the "you" that maybe you've never discovered or didn't even know existed.

PART ONE

Recognizing the Problem

CHAPTER ONE

THE EMOTIONAL BURDEN
YOU CARRY

There was a little girl who had a little curl right in the
middle of her forehead and when she was good she was
criticized anyway.
      —Elan Golomb, Ph.D., *Trapped in the Mirror*[1]

For many years, wherever I went, I was accompanied by a gang of
harsh critics who made my life almost unbearable. No matter
what I tried to accomplish, they were always there reminding me that
I wasn't up to the task and could never do a good enough job. If I was
in the midst of spring-cleaning or working hard on a home improve-
ment project, they screamed at me, "This house will never be what
you want it to be." While I was exercising, they would nag, "It doesn't
matter how hard you try; your body is falling apart, and you're a
wimp. Can't you lift more weights than that?" I'd make financial decisions, and they would bark at me, "You were always a moron at
math, and now you're a mess at finances!" My internal critics were
particularly nasty when it came to my relationships with men, whis-
pering things like "Can't you see you're a loser? You always pick the
wrong men. Why don't you just give up?" And most hurtful of all,
when I was having problems with my children, they would stridently
announce, "Your life choices have harmed your children; you should
be ashamed of yourself!"

These incessantly disapproving voices never gave me a moment's peace. They harangued, nagged, and demeaned me with the overall message that no matter how hard I tried, I could never succeed, could never be good enough. They created such an extreme sensitivity in me that I constantly assumed others were judging me as critically as I was judging myself.

Finally I realized that these "critics" were destroying me emotionally, and I made a decision to annihilate them—it was a question of my very survival. Fortunately, my decision led to my recovery, as well as my research, clinical work, and the writing of this book.

After I decided that the inner critics had to go, my first order of business was to figure out where they had originated. As a psychotherapist, I figured they were probably connected to my family history, but my background didn't seem problematic. My family touted a sturdy Dutch, German, Norwegian, and Swedish heritage with a solid work ethic with no overly mean personalities or apparent child abuse. My self-protecting denial reminded me that I had grown up with a roof over my head, clothes to wear, food to eat. So what was my problem? I promised myself I would find out.

Why Am I So Unsure of Myself?

For 28 years I had conducted psychotherapy with hundreds of women and families, which provided me with clinical experience to draw from as I sought to unravel my own internal mystery. I had treated scores of women who shared many of the same symptoms I was finally recognizing within myself: oversensitivity, indecisiveness, self-consciousness, lack of self-trust, inability to succeed in relationships, lack of confidence regardless of our accomplishments, and a general sense of insecurity. Some of my clients had spent unproductive years in therapy with other practitioners, or had purchased stacks of self-help books that never seemed to pinpoint what was causing their pain. My clients ranged from high-powered, successful professionals and CEOs to stay-at-home soccer moms to drug-addicted mothers on welfare to public figures. Like me, my clients had always felt that they lacked something crucial in their lives that seemed to be connected to the distorted self-image and insecurity that haunted their adult lives. Like me, they felt they were never good enough:

- "I'm always second-guessing myself. I replay a conversation repeatedly, wondering how I could have handled it differently or just to bask in my shame. Most of the time I realize there is no logical reason for me to feel embarrassed, but I still feel that way. I'm really anxious about what other people think of me" (Jean, 54).

- "People often compliment me on my accomplishments—my master's degree in communications, my successful public relations career, the children's book I wrote—but I can't seem to allow myself the credit I probably deserve. Instead, I beat myself up for what I think I've done poorly or should have done better. I'm such a cheerleader for my friends; why can't I be that way for myself?" (Evelyn, 35).

- "When I die, I've told my husband he can carve my tombstone with, 'She tried, she tried, she tried, she tried, and then she died' " (Susan, 62).

After years of study and clinical work, I began to see that the debilitating symptoms I shared with so many of my female clients had their origin in a psychological problem called narcissism—specifically, our mothers' narcissism. Much of what I had read regarding narcissism pertained to men, but when I looked at descriptions of it, something clicked. I realized that there are mothers who are so emotionally needy and self-absorbed that they are unable to give unconditional love and emotional support to their daughters. I saw that my clients' troubled relationships with their mothers, as well as my own relationship with mine, were clearly connected to maternal narcissism.

It became clear to me that the crucial element missing in my own life and in the lives of my insecure, unfulfilled female clients was the nurturing and empathetic love that we all desperately needed—but didn't get—from our mothers. And our mothers probably hadn't gotten it from their mothers, either, which means that a painful legacy of distorted love was passed from generation to generation. The more I learned about narcissism and how it plays out in the mother-daughter relationship, the more completely I committed myself to helping instill understanding, self-trust, and self-love in the daughters of narcissistic mothers.

This book is designed to explain the dynamic of maternal narcissism—and to provide you with strategies to overcome it—without in any way blaming narcissistic mothers. Healing comes from understanding and love, not blame. When we can understand the barriers to love that our mothers faced, which resulted in their inability to give us love, we can begin to take steps to ensure our own well-being. Your goal is to understand and to take responsibility for yourself and to heal.

In this book, you will learn to be loving toward yourself and also your mother. In the beginning stages of this process, you might feel deeply hurt, sad, angry, and even enraged. These reactions are normal, a critical step on the road to recovery. In time, as you gain more understanding of maternal narcissism, you will be able to embrace a new kind of love to replace the distorted love you received as the daughter of a narcissistic mother.

Why Focus on Mothers and Daughters?

Both boys and girls suffer emotional disruptions when a narcissistic father or mother raises them. A mother, however, is her daughter's primary role model for developing as an individual, lover, wife, mother, and friend, and aspects of maternal narcissism tend to damage daughters in particularly insidious ways. Because the mother-daughter dynamic is distinctive, the daughter of a narcissistic mother faces unique struggles that her brothers don't share.

A narcissistic mother sees her daughter, more than her son, as a reflection and extension of herself rather than as a separate person with her own identity. She puts pressure on her daughter to act and react to the world and her surroundings in the exact manner that Mom would, rather than in a way that feels right for the daughter. Thus, the daughter is always scrambling to find the "right" way to respond to her mother in order to win her love and approval. The daughter doesn't realize that the behaviors that will please her mother are entirely arbitrary, determined only by her mother's self-seeking concern. Most damaging is that a narcissistic mother never approves of her daughter simply for being herself, which the daughter desperately needs in order to grow into a confident woman.

A daughter who doesn't receive validation from her earliest relationship with her mother learns that she has no significance in the world and her efforts have no effect. She tries her hardest to make a genuine connection with Mom, but fails, and thinks that the problem of rarely being able to please her mother lies within herself. This teaches the daughter that she is unworthy of love. The daughter's notion of mother-daughter love is warped; she feels she must "earn" a close connection by seeing to Mom's needs and constantly doing what it takes to please her. Clearly, this isn't the same as feeling loved. Daughters of narcissistic mothers sense that their picture of love is distorted, but they don't know what the real picture would look like. This early, learned equation of love—pleasing another with no return for herself—has far-reaching, negative effects on a daughter's future romantic relationships, which we'll see in a later chapter.

What Is Narcissism?

The term narcissism comes from Greek mythology and the story of Narcissus. Narcissus was handsome, arrogant, and self-involved—and in love with his own image. He couldn't tear himself away from his reflection in a pool of water to become involved with anyone else, and ultimately his self-love consumed him. He died gazing at himself in the water. In everyday usage, a narcissist is someone who is arrogantly self-absorbed. Self-love or self-esteem, on the other hand, has come to mean a healthy appreciation and regard for oneself that does not preclude the ability to love others.

The *Diagnostic and Statistical Manual of Mental Disorders (DSM)* describes narcissism as a personality disorder classified by the nine traits listed below. Narcissism is a spectrum disorder, which means it exists on a continuum ranging from a few narcissistic traits to the full-blown narcissistic personality disorder. The American Psychiatric Association estimates that there are approximately 1.5 million American women with narcissistic personality disorder. Even so, nonclinical narcissism is a more pervasive problem. In truth, we all have some of these traits, and those at the low end of the spectrum are perfectly normal. However, as you go farther along the spectrum of narcissism, you encounter more problems.

Here are the nine traits of narcissism, including examples of how they present themselves in the mother-daughter dynamic. The narcissistic personality:

1. Has a grandiose sense of self-importance, e.g., exaggerates achievements and talents, expects to be recognized as superior without commensurate achievements.

(Example: The mother who can talk only about herself and what she's involved in, and never asks her daughter about herself.) Sally hates to introduce people to her mother because her mother never stops talking about her volunteer work at Children's Hospital, giving medical descriptions as though she herself is the doctor. To hear her talk, she has saved many lives!

2. Is preoccupied with fantasies of unlimited success, power, brilliance, beauty or ideal love.

(Example: The mother who believes her career cleaning houses will bring her widespread recognition through the efforts of her famous clients.) Mary's mother constantly talks about her "important" clients and how much they need her and appreciate her and how she believes she will be hired on a movie set with one of them soon.

3. Believes that he or she is "special" and unique and can only be understood by, or should associate with, other special or high-status people (or institutions).

(Example: The mother who takes her family out to dinner and treats the waitstaff like serfs in her personal kingdom.) Carrie says it is embarrassing to go out to dinner as a family when her mother comes along because she truly acts like she is the "queen of the lizard lounge."

4. Requires excessive admiration.

(Example: The mother who demands praise, gratitude, and compliments for everything she's ever done for you.) Jane's mother attends her grandson's soccer games every once in a while, but when she does, she expects Jane and her family to appreciate the fact that she sacrificed her time in order to be there. She is forever bringing up "all that I do for you kids!"

5. Has a sense of entitlement, i.e., unreasonable expectations of especially favorable treatment or automatic compliance with his or her expectations.

(Example: The mother who feels too important to stand in line.) Marcy's mother liked to gamble, but when she went to casinos she immediately got a wheelchair, though she was clearly not disabled, so that she could be pushed to the front of the line. In grocery stores, Marcy's mother would stand in the middle of the aisle and ask perfect strangers, "Could you find this for me?"

6. Is interpersonally exploitative, i.e., takes advantage of others to achieve his or her own ends.

(Example: The mother who seeks out only "friends" who can help her get somewhere with her own goals in life.) Sarah's mother talks about her friends in terms of what they can do for her, as opposed to their likable qualities. Her mother recently rejected a longtime friend when the friend was diagnosed with lupus. The mother was afraid her friend would need something from her.

7. Lacks empathy: is unwilling to recognize or identify with the feelings and needs of others.

(Example: The mother who immediately restates any story her daughter has told, pointing out the correct way to tell it.) Candace cannot really speak at all in her mother's presence without being corrected, criticized, or demeaned in some way.

8. Is often envious of others or believes that others are envious of her.

(Example: The mother who says she has no female friends because "most women are jealous of me.") Sue's mother believes she is gorgeous and therefore a threat to other women. She often repeats the old L'Oréal commercial in which the beautiful model proclaims, "Don't hate me because I'm beautiful."

9. Shows arrogance, haughty behaviors or attitudes.

(Example: The mother who believes that her children are too good to play with other children who have fewer material luxuries.) Jackie's mother allowed her to associate only with children from moneyed families because most people were not "good enough" for her well-heeled children.[2]

Each of these nine traits is exhibited through behaviors that say "It's all about me" and "You're not good enough." Narcissists lack empathy and are unable to show love. They appear to have a superficial emotional life, and their world is image-oriented, concerned with how things look to others. If your mother exhibits many of the above narcissistic traits, you may usually feel that she doesn't really know you because she never takes the time to focus on who you really are. We daughters of narcissistic mothers believe we have to be there for them—and that it is our role to attend to their needs, feelings, and desires—even as young girls. We don't feel that we matter to our mothers otherwise.

Without empathy and love from her mother, a daughter lacks a true emotional connection and therefore feels that something is missing. Her essential emotional needs are unmet. In severe cases of maternal narcissism, where neglect or abuse is involved, the most basic level of parental care is missing. In more subtle cases, daughters grow up feeling empty and bereft and don't understand why. My goal is to help you understand why you feel as you do and free you to feel better.

When Mothers Don't Bond with Their Daughters

As we grow through each stage of development, when our parents nurture and love us, we grow up feeling secure—our emotional needs are being met. But when a daughter does not receive this nurturing, she grows up lacking emotional confidence and security, and must figure out a way to gain these by herself—not an easy task when she doesn't know why she always feels empty to begin with.

Normally, a mother interacts with her baby and responds to her every movement, utterance, and need. She thus fosters a solid bond of trust and love. The child learns to trust her mother to provide her with physical necessities, emotional warmth, compassion, and approval, which allows her to develop self-reliance. But a mother without compassion, who fails to forge a bond with her daughter, provides for that daughter only when it is in the mother's best interest. Her daughter thus learns that she can't depend on her mother. She grows up apprehensive, worried about abandonment, expecting deceit at every turn.

A striking example of the effect of maternal narcissism is exemplified in a dream told to me by my client Gayle. The dream has recurred throughout her lifetime, beginning when she was a child and continuing into her adult life.

> I'm dancing through a summery green meadow carpeted with delicate wildflowers and shaded with stately trees. There's a melodic brook whispering through the tall grass. In a clearing, I spy a beautiful, spirited mare, a flawlessly white horse, which is grazing, unperturbed by my approach. I run to her joyously, anticipating her whinny of appreciation and approval as I offer the apple I pick from a nearby grove. She ignores me and the fruit and viciously bites my shoulder instead, then returns to her foraging with complete indifference.

After reporting this dream, Gayle said to me sadly, "If my own mother can't love me, who can?" Gayle came to understand that the horse in the dream represented her longing for a fantasy mother, the one she wished she had, as well as her real mother, who typically turned away and did not respond to her needs for love and approval.

It's a natural human feeling to long for a mother who loves everything about you absolutely and completely. It's normal to want to lay your head on your mother's breast and feel the security and warmth of her love and compassion. To imagine her saying, "I'm here for you, baby," when you reach out for her. We all need more than the roof over our head, food to eat, and clothes to wear: We need the unconditional love of a trusted, loving parent.

My sixty-year-old client, Betty, reported that she still wishes she had a good mother but pragmatically gave up on that a long time ago. "I used to cry myself to sleep wishing I just had that mother to love me and make me a pot of soup."

Cerena, a beautiful thirty-year-old friend of my daughter, was chatting with me one day about her mother and also telling me about her therapy. She encapsulated the longing for maternal love in her statement "When I am talking to my therapist, sometimes I want to jump into her lap, curl up on the couch with her, and pretend she is the mommy I never had."

The feelings expressed by Gayle, Betty, and Cerena typify the longing for maternal love that daughters of narcissistic mothers experience. As you learn more about maternal narcissism and how to recover from its effects, you'll gain a healthy appreciation and love for yourself and know how to fill that old emotional void.

Hello, Hope . . . Good-bye, Denial

Motherhood is still idealized in our culture, which makes it especially hard for daughters of narcissistic mothers to face their past. It's difficult for most people to conceive of a mother incapable of loving and nurturing her daughter, and certainly no daughter wants to believe that of her own mother. Mother's Day is this country's most widely observed holiday, celebrating an unassailable institution. A mother is commonly envisioned as giving herself fully to her children, and our culture still expects mothers to tend to their families unconditionally and lovingly, and to maintain an enduring emotional presence in their lives—available and reliable no matter what.

Even though this idealized expectation is impossible for most mothers to meet, it places mothers on a heroic pedestal that discourages criticism. It is therefore psychologically wrenching for any child—or adult child—to examine and discuss her mother frankly. It is especially difficult for daughters whose mothers don't conform at all to the saintly maternal archetype. Attributing any negative characteristic to Mom can unsettle our internalized cultural standards. Good girls are taught to deny or ignore negative feelings, to conform to society's and their family's expectations. They're certainly discouraged from admitting to negative feelings about their own mothers. No daughter wants to believe her mother to be callous, dishonest, or selfish.

I believe almost all mothers harbor good intentions toward their daughters. Unfortunately, some are incapable of translating those intentions into the kind of sensitive support that daughters need to help them through life. In an imperfect world, even a well-meaning mother can be flawed and an innocent child unintentionally harmed.

Once we daughters begin to face the painful truth that maternal narcissism does indeed exist, we can start to address the disturbing emotional patterns that we have developed throughout our lives. You can courageously look at your past and heal from it by honestly facing up to these tough questions:

- Why do I feel unlovable?
- Why do I never feel good enough?
- Why do I feel so empty?
- Why do I always doubt myself?

You can feel better and find a better way to live. You can understand what maternal narcissism did to you and decide to nurture yourself and feel good about who you are, in spite of it. You can also prevent your own children from undergoing what you went through. Every woman deserves to feel worthy of love. It is my hope that as you come to understand how narcissistic mothers treat their daughters, and as you gain support from the stories and advice you read, you will acquire the strength to break free from the longing for a mother you never had. Instead, you will be able to nurture and love the woman you have become.

So, before you proceed further, please answer the questions in the survey that follows so that you have a clearer idea of the extent of your own mother's narcissism. Even if your mother does not have all nine traits of a fully blown narcissistic personality disorder, her narcissism has no doubt hurt you.

Questionnaire: Does Your Mother Have Narcissistic Traits?

Mothers with only a few traits can negatively affect their daughters in insidious ways. (Check all those that apply to your relationship with your mother—now or in the past.)

1. When you discuss your life issues with your mother, does she divert the discussion to talk about herself?
2. When you discuss your feelings with your mother, does she try to top the feelings with her own?
3. Does your mother act jealous of you?
4. Does your mother lack empathy for your feelings?
5. Does your mother support only those things you do that reflect on her as a good mother?
6. Have you consistently felt a lack of emotional closeness with your mother?
7. Have you consistently questioned whether or not your mother likes you or loves you?
8. Does your mother do things for you only when others can see?
9. When something happens in your life (accident, illness, divorce), does your mother react with how it will affect her rather than how you feel?
10. Is your mother overly conscious of what others think (neighbors, friends, family, coworkers)?
11. Does your mother deny her own feelings?
12. Does your mother blame things on you or others rather than own responsibility for her own feelings or actions?
13. Is your mother hurt easily and does she carry a grudge for a long time without resolving the problem?
14. Do you feel you were a slave to your mother?
15. Do you feel you were responsible for your mother's ailments or sickness (headaches, stress, illness)?

16. Did you have to take care of your mother's physical needs as a child?
17. Do you feel unaccepted by your mother?
18. Do you feel your mother is critical of you?
19. Do you feel helpless in the presence of your mother?
20. Are you shamed often by your mother?
21. Do you feel your mother knows the real you?
22. Does your mother act like the world should revolve around her?
23. Do you find it difficult to be a separate person from your mother?
24. Does your mother want to control your choices?
25. Does your mother swing from egotistical to depressed mood?
26. Does your mother appear phony to you?
27. Did you feel you had to take care of your mother's emotional needs as a child?
28. Do you feel manipulated in the presence of your mother?
29. Do you feel valued by your mother for what you do, rather than for who you are?
30. Is your mother controlling, acting like a victim or martyr?
31. Does your mother make you act different from how you really feel?
32. Does your mother compete with you?
33. Does your mother always have to have things her way?

Note: All of these questions relate to narcissistic traits. The more questions you checked, the more likely your mother has narcissistic traits and this has caused some difficulty for you as a daughter and an adult.

CHAPTER TWO

The Empty Mirror

MY MOTHER AND ME

> An adult woman can hunt for and find her own value. She can graduate herself into importance. But during the shaky span from childhood to womanhood, a girl needs help in determining her worth—and no one can anoint her like her mother.
>
> —Jan Waldron,
> *Giving Away Simone*[1]

When you grow up in a family where maternal narcissism dominated, as an adult you go through each day trying your hardest to be a "good girl" and do the right thing. You believe that if you do your best to please people, you'll earn the love and respect you crave. Still, you hear familiar inner voices delivering negative messages that weaken your self-respect and confidence.

If you are a daughter of a narcissistic mother, you likely have heard the following internalized messages repeatedly throughout your life:

- I'm not good enough.
- I'm valued for what I do rather than for who I am.
- I'm unlovable.

Because you have heard such self-negating messages year after year—messages that are the result of inadequate emotional nurturing when you were little:

- You feel emptiness inside, and a general lack of contentment.
- You long to be around sincere, authentic people.
- You struggle with love relationships.
- You fear you will become like your mother.
- You worry about being a good parent.
- You have great difficulty trusting people.
- You feel you had no role model for being a healthy, well-adjusted woman.
- You sense that your emotional development is stunted.
- You have trouble being a person separate from your mother.
- You find it difficult to experience and trust your own feelings.
- You feel uncomfortable around your mother.
- You find it difficult to create an authentic life of your own.

Even if you experience only a few of these feelings, that's a lot of anxiety and discomfort to carry around. As you learn more about the mother-daughter dynamic associated with maternal narcissism, it will become clear to you how you came to feel as you do.

My research into maternal narcissism identified ten common relationship issues that occur between mothers and daughters when the mother is narcissistic. You may relate to all or only some of these issues, depending on where your mother falls on the maternal narcissism spectrum, from a few traits to the full-blown narcissistic personality disorder.

Let's take a look at these ten mother-daughter dynamics associated with maternal narcissism, which I refer to as "the ten stingers." To help us better understand how these dynamics get played out in real life, I've illustrated them with clinical examples from my practice as well as instances from popular culture.

The Ten Stingers

1. You find yourself constantly attempting to win your mother's love, attention, and approval, but never feel able to please her.

Both big and little girls want to please their mothers and feel their approval. Beginning early in life, it is important for children to receive attention, love, and approval—but the approval needs to be for *who they are as individuals,* not for what their parents want them to be. But narcissistic mothers are highly critical of their daughters, never accepting them for who they are.

- If Madison Avenue ever needed to come up with a commercial aimed at daughters of narcissistic mothers, my client Jennifer could have provided them with the perfect image. During our first session, she told me that she felt like standing on a street corner holding a sign that read "Will Work for Love." Jennifer recalled always trying hard to please her mother, but one story from her childhood was particularly telling. One day in a department store, she watched her mother hold a beautiful little coin purse and understood how much her mother wanted it. She vowed somehow to get it for her, even though she was only eight years old and it was expensive. She skipped lunches at school for weeks on end until she had saved enough money to buy the elegant purse for her mom. She wrapped it in shiny red paper and saved the surprise for Christmas. On Christmas morning, she eagerly awaited her mother's reaction to the gift, but was crushed when her mom accused her of stealing it and threw it across the room, screaming, "I don't want a gift from a thief!"

- Mindy describes herself as a "messy type" and her mother as "Ms. Anal Retentive—a clean freak." She told me, "I tried for years to be clean and organized to get her approval, but I am not like her. I am right-brained. I try to keep things organized and neat, but clutter happens to me against my will. I guess I'm the creative type, and she didn't like that. I'm now fifty years old, and still when Mom comes to visit, she can't withhold her disapproval if the newspapers are scattered across the living room floor."

- Lynette never could get her mother's approval. Her mom was an accomplished pianist, and Lynette strove to be just like her. Although she spent years studying piano and giving recitals, she could never live up to her mom's expectations. "Mom still clucks when I make mistakes," she told me. Lynette decided that maybe her choice of boyfriend would finally do the trick. "When I met my husband, I thought to myself, Wait till she meets this guy. She'll love him and be happy that I chose him. I was hoping that she would adore him and that would finally give me the approval I needed. But after meeting him, she actually asked me if I thought he was cute, because she thought he looked a little rough around the edges and not as refined as she had hoped."

- Bridget remembers giving her mother gifts to prove her love. She felt particularly sad about a Mother's Day plaque she gave her mom, with the phrase "World's Best Mom" printed on it. "Mom really didn't like it. She hung it up for a while and then took it down and gave it back to me. Mom said it didn't fit her decor when she redecorated her kitchen. I still have it. I just gave up after a while."

2. *Your mother emphasizes the importance of how it looks to her rather than how it feels to you.*

"It's much better to look good than to feel good" could easily be a narcissistic mother's mantra. Looking good to friends, family, and neighbors, rather than feeling good inside, is what's most important to her. A narcissistic mother sees you as an extension of herself, and if you look good, so does she. It may appear on the surface that she is concerned about you, but at the end of the day it is really all about her and the impression she makes upon others. How you look and act is important to her only because it reflects her own tenuous self-worth. Whenever you are not on display and can't be seen by others, you become less visible to her. Sadly, how you feel inside is not really important to her.

- Twenty-eight-year-old Constance tells me, "My mother is involved in every aspect of my life: how skinny I am, the clothes I wear, the right hair color, even my career. I've never been fat, but she put me on diet pills when I was 12 and started doing my makeup for me when I was 15, explaining, 'Men leave women who let themselves go.' When I disagree with her taste, she demeans and criticizes me. Even now as an adult, when I go home I make sure to have my 'mother look' in place. I starve myself for two weeks before the visit to be thin enough."

- Gladys reported moments in her childhood when her mother tried to be a good mom. "But she could never just put her arms around me to comfort me. One time I had lost out on an audition for a high school play, and I felt sorely dejected. I just needed a hug. I think she felt bad for me, but she couldn't tune in to my feelings. Instead, she did the strangest thing. She went out and bought me some go-go boots and proudly announced that if I felt bad inside, at least I could look good the next day at school. Now I wonder if she was the one who was embarrassed that I lost the audition."

3. *Your mother is jealous of you.*
    Mothers are usually proud of their children and want them to shine. But a narcissistic mother may perceive her daughter as a threat. You may have noticed that whenever you draw attention away from

your mother, you'll suffer retaliation, put-downs, and punishments. A narcissistic mother can be jealous of her daughter for many reasons: her looks, material possessions, accomplishments, education, and even the girl's relationship with her father. This jealousy is particularly difficult for her daughter, as it carries a double message: "Do well so that Mother is proud, but don't do too well or you will outshine her."

- Samantha has always been the petite one in the family. She says that most of her relatives are overweight, including her mother, who is obese. When Samantha was 22, her mother ripped her clothes out of the closet and threw them to the bedroom floor, exclaiming, "Who can wear a size four these days? Who do you think you are? You must be anorexic, and we'd better get you some help!"

- Felice, 32, told me, "My mother always wanted me to be pretty, but not too pretty. I had a cute little waist, but if I wore a belt that defined my waistline, she told me I looked like a slut."

- Mary sadly reported, "Mom tells me I'm ugly, but then I am supposed to go out there and be drop-dead gorgeous! I was a homecoming queen candidate and Mom acted proud with her friends but punished me. There's this crazy-making message: The real me is ugly, but I am supposed to fake it in the real world? I still don't get it."

- When Addie was in high school, she was interested in a modeling career and started to investigate modeling schools and programs. She landed some fun modeling jobs for local department stores and was very excited to be doing something she loved. Her mother's jealousy, however, got in the way of Addie's dreams. Mom got on the Internet, found some over-forty beauty contests, and asked Addie to enter her in them. Addie did so, and Mom won one of the contests. The next year's family Christmas card was a picture of Mom in the beauty contest with a blurb she'd written about never being too old to do what you want in life. Addie never said anything to her mom but was deeply disappointed and embarrassed. She never followed through with her own ambition to pursue a modeling career, because the competition with her mother felt too overwhelming. When recalling this incident in therapy, Addie said sadly, "It never got to be about me."

- Laura, 50, was the youngest daughter in the family and had a close relationship with her father. "But Mom didn't want me to be around him; it was like she was jealous of our relationship because she always needed the focus to be on her! She used to say things like, 'You love your father and not me, and you will do anything for your father.' " I think that what Laura's mom really meant was that she felt threatened by the attention that her husband was showing their daughter. Laura told me that her mother once threw rocks at her and her father while they were planting flowers together in the yard.

4. *Your mother does not support your healthy expressions of self, especially when they conflict with her own needs or threaten her.*
When children are growing up, they need to be able to experience new things and learn to make decisions about what they like and don't like. This is partly how we develop a sense of self. When mothers are narcissistic, they control their child's interests and activities so that they revolve around what the mothers find interesting, convenient, or nonthreatening. They do not encourage what their daughters truly want or need. This can even extend to a daughter's decision to have a child of her own.

- In the movie *Terms of Endearment,* the family is at the dinner table when the daughter announces that she is pregnant. Her mother screams and runs from the room, saying that she is not ready to be a grandmother. Clearly, the daughter's pregnancy is not about her—it's all about her mother![2]

- Like the daughter in the film, Jeri's ability to express herself was inhibited by her mother's inability to see beyond her own needs. Jeri was always artistic as a child and began winning awards for her art in the third grade. Later she won an award for a painting that included a full scholarship to an art school, but she never took advantage of it. "I never got to use the scholarship," Jeri told me, "because my mother didn't want to drive me to the school. She thought it was a hassle."

- Ruby longed to be involved in various school activities, but when she got the lead in the school musical, her mother was furious. "You don't have time to go to all of those rehearsals! You won't be able to get everything else done around here," she screamed. Her mother made Ruby do all the household chores each day before she could even begin her schoolwork, let alone memorize her lines in the play. Ruby's mother gave her a hard time throughout the rehearsal period of the play, but when the night of the performance came around and Ruby did a good job in spite of her mother, Mom threw a huge party for her own friends to celebrate "my daughter the star." Yet none of Ruby's friends were invited to the party and Ruby's mother somehow forgot to tell her she did a good job.

- A mother can feel so threatened by her daughter's success that she won't even bring herself to attend a graduation. Maria told me that her mom gave the excuse that she couldn't attend Maria's college graduation because it was too hot that day. Maria wasn't surprised; her mother had never shared any of the trust fund money left by Maria's late father but had used it on herself, rather than helping her daughter pay for college as her father had intended. "I had to work my ass off to put myself through college and never got a dime from her," Maria told me.

5. *In your family, it's always about Mom.*

Even though "It's all about Mom" is one of the central themes throughout this book, I've added this stinger here to illustrate some specific examples of how this plays out in the mother-daughter connection. Narcissistic mothers are so self-absorbed that they don't recognize how their behavior affects other people, particularly their own children. My own mother recently acted out this fifth dynamic, but this time I knew how to handle it. While I was in the midst of deadlines writing this book, my mom wanted me to come visit her and my dad in their new home. Not only had they just recently visited me in our home, but, as I had explained to her, this was a very busy time for me writing as well as running a full-time practice. I made it clear to her that a better time for me would be after I'd completed more work on the book. She responded with, "We all have goals and some of them don't get done. You need to start doing some things that ordinary people do." In other words, it didn't matter what important things were going on in my life at the moment; it was all about what she wanted me to do: visit her. In years past, I would have done what my mom wanted me to do regardless of how it worked for me, my schedule or my finances. Thank God for recovery! This time around I held my ground and told her I'd visit when the time was right.

- Sophie was very relieved after seeing her doctor about her depression, which had lasted for months and was affecting every aspect of her life. The doctor had started her on antidepressants, and for the first time in a long time she hoped that she would be feeling better soon. She told her mother that she was about to try Prozac and showed her the prescription bottle. Her mother grabbed the bottle and threw away the pills, saying, "How could you do this to me? Have I been that bad a mother?"

- "It's all about Mom" can play out in fairly obvious displays of maternal competition. Penny's mother usurped the spotlight that normally would have been on the daughter before her wedding. "I had seen a beautiful silver sugar bowl and creamer at a local shop, and told my family that I planned to buy these items with the wedding money we had received. But when I went back to the store the following week to buy the set, it was gone. I thought nothing more about it until Christmas morning, when I was opening presents with my family. My mother had gotten a gift of that very sugar bowl and creamer from my dad. Turns out she had sent him to the shop I'd told them about—to get it for her. Then to top it off, she used the silver set to upstage me at a pre-wedding party. In the South it is customary before the wedding to have a tea and set up a table to show off your wedding gifts. My mother actually arranged a display table of her own. After people looked at my table, my mother would say, 'Now come here and look at the really beautiful sugar and creamer I got.' She never realized how her competitiveness affected me." Penny's mother goes to elaborate lengths to demonstrate that it's all about her.

- Patricia's mother is from New York and has that city's distinctive accent. "Whenever she doesn't want to talk about something I bring up because she really wants to talk about herself, she will give me this certain look and say 'What eva' and then go directly into a diatribe about *her* situation or feelings." Patricia's mother's two-word phrase is quick and cutting.

- Even an infant's behavior can be misconstrued by a narcissistic mother who sees everything in terms of how it affects her. In the film *Pieces of April*, the mother (Patricia Clarkson) describes how she hates her daughter, April (Katie Holmes). She says, "She even bit my nipples when I breast-fed her."[3] *Oh, Mommy,* we imagine the infant girl saying. *I didn't mean to, I was only a few months old!*

6. *Your mother is unable to empathize.*

Lack of empathy is a trademark of narcissistic mothers. When a daughter grows up with a mother who is incapable of empathy, she feels unimportant; her feelings are invalidated. When this happens to a young girl, an older girl, or even a grown woman, she often gives up talking about herself or tuning in to her own feelings.

- Alice was distraught over her divorce, and her mother constantly pressed her for details, which didn't help. She would ask Alice, "Who's getting the house? What about custody issues? Which attorney did you hire?" Reluctantly, Alice answered all her mother's questions, but when she tried to express how the divorce was making her feel, her mother would have none of it. Instead, she focused on how much alimony Alice should ask for and what her attorney should be doing. Unable to tune in to Alice's emotional pain, her mother made her daughter feel unimportant. Alice kept asking herself, "But what about how I feel? Do I matter?"

- Throughout the 1990 movie *Postcards from the Edge*, the daughter, Suzanne (Meryl Streep), stays angry at her mother, Doris (Shirley MacLaine), who can't acknowledge or empathize with her pain. For example, when Suzanne enters drug rehab, all her mother can talk about is her hair, her makeup, and the way the room is decorated—anything but how getting off drugs must be affecting her daughter. When

Suzanne gets out of rehab, Doris throws a party, ostensibly for her daughter, but invites only her own friends. At the party, the schism between mother and daughter is further highlighted when Doris asks Suzanne to sing a song, and she chooses "You Don't Know Me." Doris then upstages and humiliates her daughter by singing the song "I'm Here"—obviously referring to how she was there for her daughter during her awful year of rehab. At this infamous party, Suzanne finally sings, "I'm checkin' out of this heartbreak hotel." [4] Checking out of her mother's world, in which empathy was nonexistent, is exactly what this daughter needed to do.

I remember a point in my own recovery from maternal narcissism when I realized fully that my mother did not want to hear about me. Still, I would persist in telephone conversations to tell her about what I was doing, rebelliously forcing her to listen. She would often wait for a break in the conversation and then turn the phone over to Dad. Sometimes I would time it, gauging how long I could talk before I got the Dad voice at the other end. Unable to empathize, she had to step aside to cede her role as parent temporarily to my father. After she broke another record in handing me over to Dad in only a few seconds, I decided not to push it further. I had my proof and there was no point in making us both feel bad.

7. *Your mother can't deal with her own feelings.*

Narcissists don't like to deal with feelings—including their own. Many daughters I've worked with grew up denying or repressing their real feelings in order to put on an act they learned their mother wanted to see. These daughters describe their mothers as going "stone cold" or "fading into the woodwork" when feelings are discussed. Some report that their mother can express only anger, which she does often. When a mother's emotional range is limited to cold, neutral, or angry, and she doesn't allow herself or her daughter to express her true feelings, the two will have a superficial relationship with very little emotional connection.

- Brenda tells me, "My mother deals with feelings like a hurricane. Everything in her path gets destroyed. She yells a lot and swears a lot. It's always everybody else's fault. She doesn't deal with her feelings."

- Helen was on a wonderful European trip after she graduated from college. She had met a guy and was thinking of marrying him. She eagerly called her mother back in the States to discuss her feelings. Mom said, "I don't want to discuss this," and hung up on her. To this day, Helen still wonders what her mother was thinking. Yet, even though Helen is in her forties now, she has never asked her mother about this emotionally charged incident. She learned early in life never to bring up "feelings" issues.

- Stacy wanted very badly to discuss her childhood with her mother, which she'd never been able to do, because her mother would get too angry. But Stacy had been in therapy and made great strides toward her own recovery. She planned to have a long talk with her parents when they were in town for a visit. This time she felt the changes she'd gone through would help her communicate differently with her mother. In her backyard, chatting about the children and the family barbecue they would have that day, Stacy mentioned to her mother that she would love to be able to speak openly with her, as she now does with her own children, but as soon as she brought up childhood feelings, her mother began to drift away and become preoccupied with weeding the garden. Rather than get angry, her mother clammed up and completely withdrew, leaving Stacy virtually alone. After an uncomfortable moment of silence, Stacy and her mother went back to talking about the food for the family get-together, as though nothing had happened. When Stacy described this to me in therapy, I asked her how it felt. She had no words, but tears fell as she sat very still for a few minutes. Then with a sigh, she said, "There is no me; there can't be with her."

Stacy saw that her mother can't deal with her own feelings or her daughter's, and that the emotional distance from her mother was truly unbridgeable.

8. *Your mother is critical and judgmental.*

It is very hard for an adult to get over being constantly criticized or judged as a child. We become overly sensitive about everything. Narcissistic mothers are often critical and judgmental because of their own fragile sense of self. They use their daughters as scapegoats for their bad feelings about themselves, and blame them for their own unhappiness and insecurity. Children—and sometimes adults—don't understand that the reason Mom is so critical is because she feels bad about herself, so instead of recognizing the criticism as unjust or a product of their mothers' frustration, they absorb it. ("I must be bad, or Mother would not be treating me like this.") These negative messages from our early upbringing become internalized—we believe them to be true—causing us great difficulties later in life. A narcissistic mother's criticisms create a deep feeling within her daughter that she is "never good enough." It is incredibly hard to shake.

- Marilyn's unique talents were overlooked by her mother, who could focus only on—and criticize—what she perceived as Marilyn's faults. Her mother was a good dancer and valued people who were "into music," particularly those who could dance well. She sent Marilyn to ballet and tap lessons as soon as she could walk and talk. But Marilyn was a singer, not a dancer. "Mom told me I was unteachable—a klutz. She would even tell this to her friends, and I remember them laughing about it. Even though I was good at singing, all she could say was, 'Too bad she can't dance.' "

- When Sharon married her third husband, she was afraid to announce the news to her parents because she knew her mother would be wary and critical. After Sharon told them the exciting news, her mother said, "I could get a spot in *Guinness World Records*. I could tell them I have only one daughter, but three sons-in-law!" Sharon cried almost the entire hour when she told me this story, and I have to admit, I cried with her.

- Ann related in therapy that she tries hard to be independent, but her mother has affected how she views the world and feels about herself. "I'm insecure about my abilities. I always sense that my mother is looking over my shoulder, and if I make the tiniest error it's like she's there judging me. Everything I do has a piece of 'What would Mom think?' in it. She's always a voice in my head."

- Chris told me that she was fearful of inviting her mother to her wedding. "Mom thinks she knows it all and is so critical and judgmental. I was afraid that during a quiet moment in the wedding she would say, 'I give them two years.' "

9. *Your mother treats you like a friend, not a daughter.*

In a healthy mother-daughter relationship, the mother acts parental and takes care of the child. The daughter should be able to rely on her mother for nurturing, not the other way around. During the child-rearing years, the two should not be friends or peers. But because mothers with narcissistic traits usually did not receive proper parenting themselves, they are like needy children inside. With their own daughters, they have a captive audience, a built-in source for the attention, affection, and love they crave. As a result, they often relate to their children as friends rather than offspring, using them to prop themselves up and meet their emotional needs. Sometimes being a supportive friend to her mother is the only way for the daughter to get positive strokes from Mom. The daughter may fall into the friend role willingly, not even realizing there is something terribly wrong with the arrangement until much later in life.

- Ever since Tracy can remember, her relationship with her mother was like being best friends. She says, "I was only 12, and I would hang out with Mom and her friends. I would cut her friends' hair, and we would all go on diets together. My mom and I were totally enmeshed. She would tell me everything about her friends, my dad and their relationship, including the sexual stuff. It didn't matter that I was uncomfortable hearing all that. She needed me to be there for her."

- Cheryl's mother was a single parent and dated constantly. When she arrived home from dates, she would tell Cheryl all about the man she dated, what they did and how she felt about him. "My mom's total life was about dating, and I had to hear about every escapade. I really wanted Mom to be into me and what I was doing, but we always had to talk about her boyfriends and her emotional life." Cheryl also said that her mother left her with a nanny most of the time and didn't bother coming to any of her school activities. "She didn't even know who I was dating or what I was involved with at school, but I knew all about her social scene."

There are many adult topics to which children should not be exposed. Children need to be allowed to be children, to focus on the things that matter to them, and they should not be burdened with adult concerns. Narcissistic parents involve their children prematurely in the adult world. A narcissistic mother who constantly confides in her daughter about difficulties in her relationship with her husband, for example, does not understand how painful this can be for her child. The daughter knows that she shares traits with her father as well as her mother, so criticizing a young child's father is like criticizing the daughter too. The daughter needs to be allowed to depend on both her parents, but when a mother shares adult concerns with her daughter, a healthy dependence becomes impossible; the daughter feels insecure and alone because she has no parent on whom she can depend. She also feels guilty about not being able to fix the parental marriage problem or her mother's issues. Again, the internal message she's left with is, "I'm not good enough [because I can't fix Mom's problems]." In part 2, we'll see how this self-negating message affects a daughter's love relationships later in life.

10. *You have no boundaries or privacy with your mother.*

Separating emotionally from your mother as you grow older is crucial to psychological growth, but a narcissistic mother does not allow her daughter to be a distinct individual. Rather, the daughter is there for her mother's needs and wishes. This creates a significant problem for the daughter. There are no boundaries, no privacy in her family life. Her mother can talk to her about anything, no matter how inappropriate—and tell other people anything about her daughter, no matter how embarrassing. The narcissistic mother usually has no clue how wrong this is, and how unhealthy it is for her daughter. To the mother, her child is simply an extension of herself.

- Cheryl's mother crossed the line when Cheryl was reconnecting with a high school friend. "I was so excited to find my friend and see what she had been up to in her adult life. We had been very close in junior high and high school and then lost touch. She had lost my number but found my parents in the directory. My mother answered her call and talked to my friend for a long time, making sure to brag to her that I was a practicing physician. But Mom was also quick to report the sordid details of my failed romances. When I finally talked to my friend, she inquired first about my relationships. I felt instant shame and embarrassment—and so violated by Mom. Why didn't she let *me* tell my friend about my life and the problems I've had so I could explain what really happened and why?"

- Marion's mother violates her actual physical space by using a key to her house and slipping in every once in a while to check up on Marion's housekeeping. She then leaves nasty notes. The last one said, "Did I really raise you to be such a slob? There could be bugs in that refrigerator! Should we use that mold to make some penicillin?"

- Ruth's mother has no boundaries when it comes to Ruth's boyfriends. "Mother hugs, kisses, and even sleeps with them if I break up with them. Once she was at my birthday party and started making out with my ex-boyfriend in front of all my friends. And she was still married! When I confronted her, she said, 'Well, he asked me to go home with him and I said no.' I told her, 'Thanks, Mom, for that consideration!' "

- In Nicole Stansbury's compelling novel, *Places to Look for a Mother*, she describes the lack of privacy when the mother, oblivious to the daughter's needs, feels she can walk into the bathroom even while the daughter is using it. The daughter says, "You always walk in the bathroom. We can never have locks. You never knock." The mother replies with, "No wonder I'm on pins and needles all day, no wonder my nerves are shot. I can't do anything, can't make a single move without being accused. I don't know what you are afraid of my seeing, what the big secret is. You don't even have *pubic* hair yet." [5] Not only does this mother fail to respect her

daughter's boundaries and privacy, she blames her
disrespectful behavior on her daughter.

In order to become a healthy, mature, independent woman, a
daughter needs to feel she has a separate sense of self, apart from her
mother. Narcissistic mothers don't comprehend this. Their own im-
maturity and unmet needs obstruct their daughters' healthy individuation, which stunts emotional development.

Where Am I in the Mirror?

Sadly, due to the detrimental effects of these ten stingers, when the
daughter of a narcissistic mother looks for her own image in the mirror, she has trouble seeing herself. Instead, her sense of self is merely
a reflection of how her mother sees her, which is too often cast in a
negative light.

Through each stage of development, daughters can't help inter-
nalizing the negative messages and feelings their narcissistic mothers
have conveyed over the years. You may have forgotten exact events or
emotional traumas, but you have likely memorized the self-defeating
messages. We daughters carry these into our adult lives: They create
unconscious emotional and behavioral patterns that cause us problems, and can be very difficult to overcome. You can silence these
messages once you understand their origin and influence and work to
formulate your own healthy beliefs about yourself. You can learn
to supplant these negative voices and change your self-image by learning more about how your mother developed her narcissistic behavior.
As we'll discover in the next chapter, a self-absorbed mother has
a vulnerable self-esteem, which causes her to project her own self-
hatred onto her daughter. Maternal narcissism takes numerous forms,
and we'll explore these different types of narcissistic mothers in
chapter 3.

THE FACES OF
MATERNAL NARCISSISM

All of life, all history happens in the body. I am learning
about the woman who carried me inside of hers.
—Sidda Walker, in
Divine Secrets of the Ya-Ya Sisterhood[1]

Self-trust, self-love, and self-knowledge can be taught to a daughter only by a mother who possesses those qualities herself. Furthermore, to pass them on successfully, a mother needs to have created an engaged and balanced relationship with her daughter. One of the problems with narcissism is that it does not allow for balance. Daughters of narcissistic mothers live in family environments that are extreme. True to their legacy of distorted love, which has been carried over from generation to generation, most narcissistic mothers either severely over-parent (the engulfing mother) or severely under-parent (the ignoring mother). Although these two parenting styles are seemingly opposite, to a child raised with either narcissistic style, the impact of the opposite is the same. Your self-image becomes distorted and feelings of insecurity seem impossible to shake.

The engulfing mother smothers, seemingly unaware of her daughter's unique needs or desires. Perhaps you were raised like this. If so, it is likely that the natural talents you had, the dreams you wanted to pursue, and maybe even the relationships most important to you were rarely nurtured. Your mother constantly sent messages to you about who she needed you to be, instead of validating who you really were. Desperate to merit her love and approval, you conformed, and in the process, lost yourself.

If you were raised by an ignoring mother, the message she gave you over and over was that you were invisible. She simply did not have enough room in her heart for you. As a result, you were dismissed and discounted. Children with severe ignoring mothers do not receive even the most basic requirements of food, shelter, clothing or protection, let alone guidance and emotional support. Lack of a consistent home environment may have made you feel insecure, unhealthy, or unsuccessful at school. Emotional and physical neglect sends you the message that you don't matter.

Having a narcissistic mother, whether she is engulfing or ignoring, makes individuation—a separate sense of self—difficult for a daughter to accomplish. Daughters with unmet emotional needs keep going back to their mothers, hoping to gain their love and respect at a later date. Daughters who have a full emotional "tank" have the confidence to separate in a healthy fashion, and move on into adulthood. Later, in the recovery chapter, we will address this in greater depth. For now, let's look at the different faces of engulfing and ignoring mothers and their effects on daughters.

The Engulfing Mother

The engulfing mother tries to dominate and control every aspect of her daughter's life. She makes all the decisions and pressures the daughter on what to wear, how to act, what to say, what to think, and how to feel. Her daughter has little room to grow and blossom individually or to find her own voice, becoming in many ways an extension of her mother.

Engulfing mothers often appear to be great moms. Because they're very involved in their daughters' lives and may always be doing things for them and with them, others outside the family often view them as active, engaged parents. Yet, the weakened self-image and the sense of unworthiness their daughters take away from this behavior are tragic. Narcissistic mothers are unaware of the damaging, often devastating consequences of their behavior, which of course does not diminish its lasting effects.

- Miriam was 28 years old, engaged to be married, and locked in a fierce struggle with her mother over control of her life. Miriam's mother did not approve of her fiancé, and was doing everything conceivable to interfere, including speaking negatively about him to several people at his place of employment. "My mother hoped the word would get back to me that my fiancé was a loser or better still, that he would give up and leave town."

- "Let me tell you a thing or two about love relationships," Toby's mother would say to her all too often. Toby, 48, describes her mother as someone who "loves men and knows how to manipulate them." When Toby was old enough to date, her mother would coach her on how to keep a man's interest, admonishing her daughter if she was not flirtatious enough. "She would undo the top buttons on my blouse, and show me how to act sexy." Toby remembers her mother's sage advice: "If you don't sleep with them, you lose them."

- Sandy's mother always wanted her daughter to be just like her. She took pride in telling people that she was trying to clone herself. When Sandy went into recovery, she felt she had to fight her entire family's perceptions that she was a younger version of her mother. "We were connected, my mother and I, but I had to ask all my relatives to please quit putting the burdens of her sins on me."

Showbiz moms are a classic example of engulfing mothers, the ones who shepherd their daughters through child beauty pageants or TV shows like *Showbiz Moms & Dads*. The ad for this show in a popular magazine contains the line "Some parents want fame so badly" next to a picture of a mother pushing her little princess onto the stage. It makes you worry about how these experiences affect the minds of these young, manipulated children, and what kind of young women they will become.

The musical *Gypsy* features the quintessential engulfing mom.[2] "Sing out, Louise," the mother says as her daughter is entertaining onstage. In the original movie version, Rosalind Russell plays Mama Rose, a flamboyant, extroverted, narcissistic mother with two daughters, Louise and June, whom she is pushing into show business. When the younger daughter, June, who Mama Rose thinks is more talented, marries and leaves home, Mama Rose, looking for another way to realize her own aspirations, focuses on the older daughter, Louise (Natalie Wood). The daughters' responses in this production are interesting. June eventually tires of being the "cute one" and runs away, and Louise rebels by becoming the famous stripper Gypsy Rose Lee. Both daughters leave their mother with her dreams unrealized.

Each one of us is imbued with a deep yearning to live our own life, not our mother's. Yet the narcissistic mother puts pressure on her child to act and react to the world as she would. A child raised in this way makes decisions according to what she believes will win her mother's love and approval. Accustomed to her mother thinking for her, the girl has difficulty later on creating an authentic, healthy adult life for herself.

The Ignoring Mother

Mothers who ignore or under-parent their daughters do not provide guidance, emotional support, or empathy. They consistently discount and deny your emotions. Even if, as my mother instilled in me, "I had a roof over my head, clothes to wear, food to eat, so what is the problem?" I was still in a lot of inner pain—as are other daughters with mothers who ignore them.

- The comedy/drama *Mermaids* portrays an irresponsible, self-absorbed mother (Cher). In this movie, everything is about Mom and her relationships, while her daughters' emotional worlds are empty. Some of the daughters' lines in this movie say it all. For example, "This is our mother. Pray for us." "Mom is many things; normal is not one of them." And, "Mom, I'm not invisible." [3]

If a girl is fortunate, she may find another adult who can help her, recognize and validate her feelings and provide some measure of guidance. This person can be an emotional lifesaver. For instance, as Marie grew up, her mother refused to teach her about some pretty essential matters. "When I started my period at age thirteen, I couldn't go to Mom. Whenever any sexual allusion came up, even on TV, she'd say, 'Don't talk to me about sex; I don't want to discuss it.' When I needed personal items, I had to call my sister or my teacher. My teacher was the one who explained menstruation to me."

In my psychotherapy practice, I've seen case after case of mothers and daughters whose relationship looks good on the outside, but inside the child is feeling deep pain, confusion, and distress. I always tell children that I am a "feelings" doctor, because I want to get the message to them right away that my office is a place to talk about feelings, which are so often ignored, devalued, or denied by their mothers. The children often learn more quickly than their parents how to discuss their feelings and to begin to heal.

Ignoring behavior creates deep emotional gaps in a child's life that can go undetected for years, but physical abuse or neglect is more blatantly visible. When narcissistic parents are unable or unwilling to meet a daughter's most basic requirements—to keep her physically safe, healthy, and in school—it shows.

My practice is full of abused and neglected kids. Working with these children has evolved as a specialty in my career, a way for me to give back and make a difference to suffering children. A piece of my heart needs to try to help little girls, especially those waiting to be adopted or who are living in foster homes, longing for mothers they don't have.

I've had many children ask me to take them home, such as one darling eight-year-old who said, "Dr. Karyl, do you know how to cook? How many bedrooms do you have at your house? Do you have any toys?" Then she quietly added, "If I can come home with you, I will do the dishes every day and even wash all your windows!" If my profession did not have certain ethical rules that preclude this, I would have opened an orphanage in my home by now. One of my respected colleagues, Linda Vaughan, who also worked with abused and ne-glected children, wrote this poem after working intensely with a foster child who had been removed from her narcissistic mother's home:

Dear Mommy
I'm doing really good,
I get all A's in school
And I don't cry at bedtime anymore,
Though my new mom said I could.
I remember how much you hate tears,
You slapped them out of me
To make me strong,
I think it worked.
I learned to use a microscope
And my hair grew two inches.
It's pretty, just like yours.
I'm not allowed to clean the house,
Only my own room,
Isn't that a funny rule?
You say kids are so much trouble
Getting born, they better pay it back.

I'm not supposed to take care
Of the other kids, only me, I sort of like it.
I still get the hole in my stomach
When I do something wrong,
I have a saying on my mirror
"Kids make mistakes, It's OK,"
I read it every day,
Sometimes I even believe it.
I wonder if you ever think of me
Or if you're glad the troublemaker's gone,
I never want to see you again.
I love you, Mommy.[4]

Sometimes these children have little to eat, live in filthy, unsanitary homes, have no medical care, or have been physically, sexually, or emotionally abused. Tragically, this sort of abuse and neglect is widespread, and although social service agencies are bad-mouthed on a daily basis, thank God they are there for these needy children.

- Madeline, an adorable ten-year-old, largely takes care of herself at home. Although she lives in a less than ideal situation, she carries a great deal of hope in her heart. "My mom never cooks meals for us. We've never had one of those family meals you see on TV where the whole family is sitting around a table and eating together. I get my own meals and I am pretty good at cans of soup and mac and cheese." One day Madeline decided to cook for her mother. She made "some pretty good" pasta and fruit cups for both of them. When little Madeline announced that dinner was ready, her mother told her that she was dieting and wasn't hungry. "So, since I had set the table with two plates," Madeline relates with a confident tilt to her head, "first I filled my plate and ate all of that, and then I switched to her plate and filled it up and ate that too. I pretended she was there. I played both people. I even had a pretend conversation with her, saying, 'Well, how was your day? What did you do today?' "

• Marion, 70, tells a horrendous story about what happened to her sister. "My older sister disappeared when she was 16. One night my brother went to pick her up from church and she wasn't there. For a year and a half we looked for her. Then one day, this semi-truck drove up and this big guy got out, followed by my sister and a baby. Then we learned my mom had run into him, he thought my sister was beautiful, he wanted her and asked how to get her. Mom said, 'Give me $300 and you can take her off my hands.' He bought her! Now my sister asks, 'Why did Mama sell me?' The guy was horrible to her, locked her in a closet while he was at work so she couldn't run away. He abused her. When my dad found out, he wanted to kill the guy, and I thought he was going to kill my mom too."

I see an astounding number of ignoring parents in divorce cases. Since the court system operates on the basis of adversarial relationships, spouses usually end up squaring off on one side or the other. Professionals advising families during divorce proceedings generally work for either the mother or the father. In many parenting-time proceedings, the discussion focuses not on what is in the best interest of the child as the law dictates, but on what is best for the parent. It is a sad commentary on our culture that many parenting-time evaluators and judges listen more intently to what the parents want than what is truly best for the children. In Denver, there is even talk about which evaluator is "for the father" and which is "for the mother." What about being a "child advocate"?

Divorce also sometimes leads one parent to turn a child against the other parent so he or she can have his way in the custody battle. This is a classic example of emotional child abuse that hurts the child much more than these alienating parents realize. In these cases, parents may take care of the child physically, but completely disregard his or her emotional needs.

- Keri's mother destroyed Keri's relationship with her father when the two adults were going through a divorce. "Mom was crazy jealous of our time with Daddy. She would say, 'Go see your father and I will be fine,' and then she would go into a depressive stupor for ten days and make us feel guilty. It got so bad that we stopped seeing Daddy because we didn't want to hurt our mom. Then he died suddenly and we couldn't even go to the funeral. We couldn't grieve his death in the presence of our mother because it bothered her too much!"

The behavior patterns of abusive, ignoring, or neglectful mothers are generally identifiable, but grow much more complex and confusing when a narcissistic mother demonstrates a mix of both engulfing and ignoring behaviors. Let's look at the ways this particular combination plays out.

The Mix of Engulfing and Ignoring Behaviors

Although my research suggests that most narcissists display one type preferentially, the two styles are not mutually exclusive. A mother can flip from engulfing to ignoring and back, as does the mother in the film *Terms of Endearment*. Aurora, the mother (Shirley MacLaine), constantly examines her infant daughter to see if she's breathing. She jiggles her baby, waking her abruptly to check. When the baby cries, Aurora indicates her maternal approval with a contented, "That's more like it," and closes the door, leaving the baby crying alone in her crib.[5]

My mother exhibited both extremes with two different daughters—engulfing behavior with my sister and ignoring behavior with me. I believe her actions were related to where we were in birth order and where Mom was in life. In a nutshell, she pressured me to grow up quickly to take care of her and help her with the rest of the family, and she tried to keep my sister a child by helping her with everything. I was the second to oldest child. My mother would say no to me and assume that I would figure things out. She would always do things for my sister, who was the baby, even when my sister was being irresponsible. While my mother gave me the message that I had to handle things on my own, she gave my sister the message that she could not handle anything without her intervention.

Effective mothering strikes a proper balance between permissiveness and restraint. A girl who has been parented on that middle ground learns she can grow along with her talents and passions; her feelings are acknowledged and treated with respect. But a girl who is raised outside that middle ground must overcome a painful set of hurdles if she wants to enjoy healthy love relationships, make satisfying career choices, and someday be an effective, affectionate, kind parent herself.

The Six Faces of Maternal Narcissism

> But enough about me. Let's talk about you. What do
> YOU think of me?
> —Bette Midler as CC Bloom in *Beaches*[6]

My research has identified six types of narcissistic mothers, all within the engulfing-ignoring spectrum. I call them "the six faces." As you explore this list, please understand that your mother can be primarily one type or a combination of several of these. In addition, the engulfing and ignoring mom can be interwoven into any of the following types.

THE FLAMBOYANT-EXTROVERT
The flamboyant-extrovert is the mother about whom movies are made. She's a public entertainer, loved by the masses, but secretly

feared by her intimate house partners and children. If you can perform in her show, too, all the better. If you can't, you'd better watch out. She is noticeable, flashy, fun, and "out there." Some love her, but you despise the outward masquerade she performs for the world. For you know that you don't really matter to her and her show, except in how you make her look to the rest of the world. Seeing how the world responds to her confuses you. You see that she doesn't offer the same warmth and charisma to you, her child, as she does to others—to friends, colleagues, family, even to strangers. "If she could only love me, then she could be whatever she wants to be and I wouldn't care," you feel. You desperately want her to know you and to let you be yourself too.

More often than not, these mothers lead charmed lives and want their daughters to fit into their social world and conform to their mold.

- Sherry's mother was a perfect example of this. She worked hard at getting attention. Her looks changed as often as the weather, and for maximum dramatic effect. "I don't recall ever seeing her natural hair color," Sherry, 55, said with a wry smile. She remembers her mother's different phases. "In the early '60s, she had the Jackie O look, big hats. When the mod things came out, she had sunglasses and miniskirts. She was always in style, the center of attention. I always felt I didn't want to move into her territory. I remember being embarrassed about the hot pants and pantyhose under them. White go-go boots and stiletto heels. She always took it a step beyond tacky. Somehow I think she knew she wasn't very authentic. She actually said she wanted this inscription on her tombstone: 'Will the real Betty please stand up?' "

- Amy had an eccentric, flamboyant mother, whose charisma helped her get into and out of a lot of interesting situations.

Her mother owned 144 pairs of shoes with matching purses and watches, and was a self-proclaimed psychic who once had her own cable TV show. A chronic liar and gossip, Amy's mother used to get together with the neighbors and give them psychic readings. "One lady on our block decided that Mom was Satan. She convinced the neighbors of that, so we got kicked out of the neighborhood. My mother's response was that people would short circuit if given too much spiritual information. She always had an excuse for things or tried to blame others."

- Lina's mother had a perfect venue in which to shine as the owner of a glamorous nightspot. Lina smiles as she recalls how every evening her mother would dress up in a ball gown and go to her coffeehouse to play hostess. A onetime blues singer who had spent time in Hollywood, Lina's mother claimed that she had sung with Desi Arnaz, partied with Frank Sinatra, and sat on Cary Grant's lap. To Lina, her mother is nothing but show. "She likes to tell people who she knows. It's all about her image. She still does inappropriate stuff like dance around the room to get attention or make an entrance that all will notice. I've always thought it was strange that when I introduced her to my friends, she would say, 'I'm so glad they got to meet me!' "

THE ACCOMPLISHMENT-ORIENTED

To the accomplishment-oriented mother, what you achieve in life is paramount. Success depends on what you do, not who you are. She expects you to perform at the highest possible level. This mom is very proud of her children's good grades, tournament wins, admission into the right college, and graduation with the pertinent degrees. She loves to brag about them too. But if you do not become what your accomplishment-oriented mother thinks you should, and accomplish what she thinks is important, she is deeply embarrassed, and may even re-spond with a rampage of fury and rage.

A confusing dynamic is at play here. Often, while the daughter is trying to achieve a given goal, the mother is not supportive because it takes away from her and the time the daughter has to spend on her. Yet if the daughter achieves what she set out to do, the mother beams with pride at the awards banquet or performance. What a mixed message. The daughter learns not to expect much support unless she becomes a great hit, which sets her up for low self-esteem and an ac-complishment-oriented lifestyle.

- As a little girl, Yasmin loved to ride horses. But her mother was reluctant to support this costly, time-consuming passion. Yasmin's father helped her, though, working hard with her to teach her barrel racing, and her mother was furious with him. But success changed the family dynamic. When Yasmin won a blue ribbon at the kids' rodeo, "Mom plastered the winning smile on her face and the bragging spree began." Yasmin remembers being confused and hurt.

- Carol grew up feeling controlled by her mother's ambition for her. She took seven years of piano lessons, where she had to play in recitals as well as for her mother's friends. "I would be playing along and hear her snort if I made a mistake. I could feel her disappointment in me. I felt like I had to be perfect for her. When I was old enough to choose, I purposely flunked the test to the academy for piano where she wanted me to go. After that, I didn't touch the piano for 12 years. When I moved out and had my own home, I wanted a piano just to play for me. I still can't play in front of Mom. When I started therapy, I had to stop playing the piano again because it brought up all the old stuff with Mom. I still have a love/hate relationship with the piano. Somehow the line between Mom's benefit and my benefit got crossed. I was a trophy for her."

- Eleanor's mother judged people solely on their educational accomplishments. First thing she always asked was where someone went to college. "Harvard and Stanford people were the very best you could find." Then she wanted to know their degree level. "M.D.'s and the Ph.D.'s were outstanding. Anything less was not good enough. All of her friends were Dr. So-and-So or married to Dr. So-and-So. She didn't care what kind of people they were or if they were even nice to her or us." Eleanor leaned back in her chair, exhaling a sigh of relief, and told me, "Thank God, I made a few A's in my day and have a couple of degrees because if not, she probably wouldn't even speak to me! Poor Dad is only at the master's level—I don't know how he survived with her."

- Mia's mother obsessed about cleaning. "She was psycho about it: Everything had to be perfect, like we clean the house before the maid comes. One thing is out of place and she notices, and becomes ballistic. She is beyond neat freak! My mom would throw out everything in my closet and make me color code my clothes. I would have to clean the bathroom four times until I did it perfectly."

- In the film *The Other Sister,* the developmentally delayed daughter says to the narcissistic mother, "Mom, you don't look at me, you don't see me, not the real me. I don't want to play tennis, or chess, or be an artist. I want to be me. I can't do those things, but *I can love.*"[7] What a powerful message.

THE PSYCHOSOMATIC

The psychosomatic mother uses illness and aches and pains to manipulate others, to get her way, and to focus attention on herself. She cares little for those around her, including her daughter, or their needs. If your mother was like this, the only way you were able to get attention from her was to take care of her. If you failed to respond to her, or even rebelled against her behavior, Mom would play the victim by becoming more ill or have an illness-related crisis to redirect your attention and make you feel guilty. I call this the "illness control method." It is very effective. If the daughter does not respond, she looks bad and feels like a loser who can't be nice to her mother. The most important thing to the psychosomatic mother is that her daughter be there to care for her and understand *her*.

Many times the psychosomatic mother uses her illnesses to escape from her feelings or from having to deal with a difficulty in life. The daughter will commonly hear from her father or other family members, "Don't tell your mother. It will upset her or make her sick." Some daughters learn that being sick themselves brings some attention from their psychosomatic mothers because illness provides a common bond. The mother can relate to illness and is able to communicate about it with the daughter, but the daughter must be careful not to be sicker than her mother is, because then the mother will not feel cared for, which she feels entitled to.

- While migraine headaches are genuinely debilitating, May's mother used them as a way of escaping problems in the household and would not take care of herself in ways that can help prevent migraines. For instance, she never dealt with her stress, a common trigger for migraines, and allowed herself to become upset by many things. "Mom was not able to deal with anything. She would instantly get a headache and have to be run to the emergency room for some shot that would knock her out for days on end. Then Dad and I would have to deal with whatever it was that was a problem. It was her escape!" This continued throughout May's young adulthood. "I remember one time telling her that I was dating a much younger man and it was like the headache came on so suddenly neither of us knew what hit her. I guess she didn't like that!"

- Irene was blamed for her mother's inability to deal with stress. "Whenever anything went wrong at home, Dad would say, 'Look what you've done to your mother.' Mom would end up in the bedroom sobbing, and have a headache and diarrhea and be on the toilet for hours and then come out to the couch with a rag on her head and all sad. Dad would come to her rescue and blame us, saying she handles stress badly." Irene needed recognition for herself, but learned that "if I don't live up to her expectations, she gets aches and pains, has cold sores on her mouth, develops weird rashes, and makes herself sick from emotional stress. Everything has to be about her."

- Jackie's mother's behavior got worse as she and Jackie's father got older and he began to get sick. "Mother always had to be sicker than Daddy was. If I gave Daddy attention because something was wrong, she always had to 'up' the illness. Once she faked a heart attack. I can't count the number of times she called me at work and I rushed over there only to find nothing wrong with her. The one time I didn't come over after a call, she didn't speak to me for days, said I never cared for her, and wrote me nasty letters."

- Mona cried during therapy as she discussed her father's hip surgery, which was hard for him because he was aging and weak. But she was really crying because "the whole time Dad was going through this, my mother said her hip hurt and she needed hip surgery too. She couldn't let the attention be on him. It was so sick! Her hips were just fine. As soon as Dad recovered, we never heard about her hips again."

- Celeste tells me, "My mom just did a lot of groaning. When she got up or sat down, or walked across the room, she just groaned! She had no physical reason to do this. It seemed to be her way of getting everyone in the room to look at her and ask her if she was okay. Then she would say, 'Of course I'm okay. Why?' "

THE ADDICTED

In Rebecca Wells's novel *Divine Secrets of the Ya-Ya Sisterhood,* Sidda describes the sound of her mother's voice as "the cacophony of five jiggers of bourbon." Although "two thousand miles apart, Sidda could hear the ice cubes clinking" as she talks to her mother on the phone. She then says, "If anyone ever made a movie about her childhood, that would be the soundtrack."[8]

The parent with a substance-abuse problem will always seem narcissistic, because the addiction speaks louder than anything else. Sometimes when an abuser sobers up, the narcissistic behavior goes away. Sometimes not. But while users are using, their focus is always on themselves and their god, the addiction. Children of alcoholics and other substance abusers know this well: The bottle or the drug of choice always comes before anything or anyone else. Substance abuse is an effective way to mask feelings. Clearly, the mother who shows up drunk at her daughter's choir concert is not thinking of her daughter's needs.

- Hanna had to fend for herself most of her childhood. "For years my mother was hooked on Tylenol with codeine and Valium—totally checked out. By the time I was ten, she had been married seven times. We moved around with lots of different men." When Hanna was 14, her mother told her that she wanted to kill herself. Hanna pleaded with her not to do it, telling her mother that "I needed her, and I couldn't survive without her." Hanna stops for a moment when she tells this story. Her pain is palpable. "She did it anyway. She died by her own hand. I always lost—first a mom who was there but not there and then a mom who killed herself." After her mother's suicide, Hanna lived in a trailer park and continued going to school. She did well until her junior year in high school, when she began to call herself in sick to school and started getting high on drugs and alcohol.

- Julia's mother was a party girl almost every night. "We lived in a neighborhood of lots of single parents when I was growing up, and they all partied. My mom loved to throw the party at our house so she didn't have to get a babysitter. I became one of those 'moral' kids. I hated the drinking, smoking, dirty stories, swearing, etc. I used to complain about it to my mom and her boyfriend. They got sick of it, so they used to humiliate me by calling me 'Queenie.' When they were planning the next party, Mom would say, 'We're having a wild party tonight, Queenie, so you can go to your room, where you won't be bothered.' "

The addicted narcissistic mother's mantra is best described by Billie Holiday: "Smoke, drink, never think."[9]

THE SECRETLY MEAN

The secretly mean narcissistic mother does not want others to know she is abusive to her children. She usually has a public self and a private self, which are quite different. Daughters of the secretly mean describe their mothers as being kind, loving, and attentive when out in public, and abusive and cruel at home. It is hard not to feel significant resentment toward your mother for this, especially if she fooled a lot of people outside the family. If you had this mother, you know how awful this inconsistent behavior feels. In church your mother has her arm around you and gives you some gum from her purse with a warm smile. At home, when you ask for the gum, or reach out to her, you get slapped and demeaned. This mother is capable of announcing in public, "I am so proud of my daughter. Isn't she beautiful?" and then saying at home, "You really should lose some weight, your hair is a mess, and you dress like a slut." These unpredictable, opposite messages are crazy-making.

- Veronica's mother was a saint in public, but angry and abusive at home. "Whatever she was feeling was the center of the universe and all life had to stop to abide by it. If she had a headache or the blues, we walked on eggshells. Her feelings dominated everything. My feelings were minimized, to put it mildly, and I learned that mine didn't hold a candle to hers. She would always say, 'If you only knew . . . You think you got it bad,' but whenever we went out somewhere, she acted all loving and really fake. Our battles were inside the home and nobody saw them."

- Robin's mother's behavior confused her. "As a kid I had always adored my mom and felt she was on my side, but when my brother and I became teenagers, she used to tell us how awful we were. 'Don't ever have children,' she would say." Robin's mother told her stories about how she tried to abort Robin by throwing herself down the stairs and taking certain drugs. "She probably would have aborted my brother," Robin tells me, "but my father was ready to be sent to war, and in those days if you were pregnant they wouldn't draft your husband." Since her mother had had three abortions and one miscarriage, she called Robin and her brother her "live births." "What was so strange, though, is that in front of others, she always talked about how she loved children and she tried so hard to have the ones she did and what a miracle we were. Huh?"

- Hailey relished the freedom of being away from her secretly mean mother after she got married. "Mom didn't like my husband, so she didn't want to see us, and it was great! Until one time I decided to go visit her. She was doing caretaking for an elderly lady in the neighborhood, and she would actually say malicious things under her breath about this poor old lady. I went out to lunch with them. The lady was hard of hearing, but it still bothered me that she would say things about this lady right in front of her. 'Do you think she could move any fucking slower?' It was so mean. It reminded me of what I had lived with my whole life. There is a nice side and a dark side of my mother. Once this older lady passes, she will project onto the rest of us again. This poor old lady is getting it now."

THE EMOTIONALLY NEEDY

While all narcissistic mothers are emotionally needy at some level, some show this characteristic more openly than others. These mothers wear their emotions on their sleeves and expect their daughters to take care of them, a losing proposition for children, who are expected to calm their mothers, listen to their adult problems, and solve problems with her. Of course, these children's feelings are neglected and you are unlikely to get anywhere near the same nurturance that you are expected to provide.

- Ivette's mother knows how to up the ante. When Ivette tells her she's tired from working all week, her mother says, "Darling, you don't know what tired is." Then her mother goes into a tirade about how exhausting *her* day was. Rarely can Ivette match her mother's story, so she just gives up telling her anything and listens. Ivette has learned not to discuss her own feelings, because it is too hurtful. "I just ask her how she is and let it go at that. She seems to get less worked up this way."

A classic example of an emotionally needy mother is portrayed in the recent film *The Mother*. In this dramatic screenplay, written by Hanif Kureishi, the daughter, Paula (Cathryn Bradshaw), feels empty, can't figure out what to do with her life and career, and has never felt loved or valued by her mother. The daughter is attracted to needy men, having been accustomed to trying to please her mother. Her self-absorbed mother, May (Anne Reid), begins to show the depth of her neediness when her husband dies, and blatantly has an affair with a carpenter, with whom the daughter is madly in love. This mother has no compassion or concern for her daughter's feelings and would have justified her actions by saying that she was grieving and the affair made her feel better. Movie critic Michael Wilmington says it well: "Self-absorption is the vice of these characters; that, not sex, is their sin." [10]

Now that you've had this inside look at many different types of narcissistic mothers, it is important to emphasize a few things. First of all, our mothers weren't born this way. They most likely faced insurmountable barriers to love and empathy when they were children. In part 3 of this book, one of your challenges will be to explore your mother's background, so that you will have a deeper understanding of the reasons for her behavior. This does not take away your pain, but allows you to empathize and forgive her to a degree that will help your recovery.

No narcissist operates in a vacuum. In the next chapter, we'll do some family study and take a look at the rest of the narcissistic nest.

CHAPTER FOUR

Where Is Daddy?

THE REST OF THE NARCISSISTIC NEST

> The narcissistic family often resembles the proverbial shiny red apple with a worm inside. It looks great, until you bite into it and discover the worm. The rest of the apple may be just fine but you've lost your appetite.
> —Stephanie Donaldson-Pressman and Robert Pressman,
> *The Narcissistic Family*[1]

The family with a narcissistic mother operates according to an unspoken set of rules. Children learn to live with those rules, but they never stop being confused and pained by them, for these rules block children's emotional access to their parents. They are basically invisible—not heard, seen, and nurtured. Tragically, conversely, this set of rules allows the parents to have no boundaries with the children and to use and abuse them as they see fit. Sounds awful, doesn't it?

Where Is Daddy?

"Daddy, why didn't you protect me? Where were you when I needed you? Why did you always have to stick up for Mom? What about me?"

These exclamations came from Marcy when we were doing an

"empty chair" exercise in therapy. She imagined her father in the empty chair, and talked to him about the family and how it hurt her to be so alone and unloved. Her questions are among those commonly put to fathers by daughters of narcissistic mothers: Where were you?

From my research and experience, the answer is clear: Father is revolving around Mother like a planet around the sun. The narcissist needs to be married to a spouse who will allow her to be at the center of all the action. That is how it has to be if the marriage is to survive. In the family drama, the narcissist is the star, and her spouse takes a supporting role.

A man gets himself into this situation for many reasons, but for our discussion the most pertinent point is that he is the kind of person who accepts this behavior from his spouse and, most of the time, enables her. Perhaps he doesn't always want to, but he does, because he has learned over time that this is what works with her. Because the father focuses on his wife, his pact with the mother can make him look narcissistic too. He is unable to attend to the needs of his daughter.

- "My father always jumped to do my mother's bidding," said forty-year-old Erica as she described her father's role during her childhood. "Mom was the boss, and Dad centered his life on her. He actually worshipped the ground she walked on. We could be watching television and a commercial would come on about ice cream. Mom would say, 'Wow, that looks good,' and Dad would head to the garage to go to the store to get it. He jumps at her command. She uses this as control in her relationship. She picks the time, and many times it's when he wouldn't typically want to go anywhere or when he is watching football. If I confront her on this, she asks, 'Does your father look unhappy?' "

- Danielle's father used to blame her for every argument she and her mother had (and there were lots of them). "If we got into an argument about cleaning my room, for example, she would be extremely emotional, end up crying, and then Dad would step in and say, 'Look what you've done. Look at how you made your mom feel!' It always became something about *her* rather than what was going on with *me*."

- Clair, 41, reports that her mother controlled the entire household, including but not limited to her father. When Mom didn't talk to her, neither did Dad. "Mom was an alcoholic, often passed out on the couch when we got home from school. I wouldn't say anything until I picked up the vibe in the house. My oldest brother finally got up the courage to tell Dad that Mom was drunk all the time. My brother looked up 'drunk' in the thesaurus and tried to make it sound better by using the word 'inebriated,' but Dad slapped him and said, 'Don't talk about your mother that way.' He always defended her."

- Carmen's father's role as his wife's protector is paramount. "In some ways, his needs don't matter either. I used to worry about that, but now I see that is what keeps them together. They need each other to play out their dysfunctional roles and survive emotionally in the world. I don't really care if that's what works for them, but it did affect me. What about me? Do I matter?" When Carmen was in recovery, she tried to talk to her mother about her upbringing. As soon as she had gotten out the words, Carmen's father jumped in to defend her mother. Carmen felt doubly discounted. Then her mother added insult to injury by saying, "Isn't he wonderful? He is the best husband anyone could ever have." Carmen said,

"The very thought that maybe this is about me—not her or her husband—would never cross either of their minds. They typically go on about how wonderful their marriage has been and how happy they are with each other. I somehow want to remind them about the many times that Dad secretly told me he wanted to run off with another woman. They just live in denial and pretend, pretend."

This unspoken agreement between parents who share a narcissistic nest is strong and impenetrable to anyone, but especially a daughter, who is seen as competition by the mother. Obviously, Carmen had gained insight from her significant recovery work, but even so, the pain of this memory still brought her to tears. Tragically, parental denial is what keeps the family together for better or worse, and many families do choose not to confront their problems even though they hurt their children. Someday Carmen will be able to tell this story and not feel the pain that was so present that day. Though she is unlikely to be able to change her parents' relationship, she can lessen its effect on her and her life.

Modeling a healthy love relationship is one of the most important things that parents do. Children who grow up with an unhealthy model are more likely to have some difficulty with love relationships as adults. Children learn far more from what they see parents do than from anything parents preach to them. In part 2, we look at the love relationships of daughters of narcissistic mothers and discuss the many effects of unhealthy parental relationships.

The emotional health of daughters of narcissistic mothers is in effect sacrificed so that their father can keep the peace with his wife. A daughter's first steps in recovery involve voicing the devastating feelings of vulnerability and helplessness this generates.

- Nineteen-year-old Kristin sadly reports, "I wonder why I was born, why did God give me to her when she didn't want me? I remember thinking I can't live through this, but I did.

I don't feel pretty, I have low self-esteem, and I can't give myself credit for things. My dad loved me and tried to protect me, but he couldn't really do it with Mom being so abusive. He had to do what she wanted to stay married to her."

- Linda, 26, reported an interesting difference between the ways her biological father and her stepfather dealt with her mom. "My stepdad has to circle his life around her, and that keeps her and them happy. He listens to her moodiness and her whining, whereas my real dad was an alcoholic and drank to numb it all out."

Most daughters report that if they did have good relationships with their fathers, their mothers were intensely jealous of them. Candace tells a heartrending story about the period when her father was dying of Parkinson's disease. "Daddy was lying on the bed in the hospital and I was lying next to him. It was truly the last hours of his life. Mom got mad that I was that close to him and asked me to move, and she then took my place next to Dad. It was sad to me because it felt like he was the only person who really loved me. Years later, we were chatting about family dynamics, and Mom informed me that she had to adjust the financial inheritance from Dad. She told me she gave me less than the other kids because I got so much from Dad when he was alive."

- Paula's father always wanted to carry her around. "I was a daddy's girl. Mom would always say, 'Put her down, let her walk,' in an angry tone. I was only about three years old and my mom was angry with me for taking my dad's attention. She wanted it all."

- Wendy and her father bonded so well that she grew up to follow in his footsteps. She also kept herself far away from her mother. She relays this story: "Mom was so jealous of my relationship with Dad. He was a medical doctor and I was in med school too. I could relate to him better, and he had empathy." Wendy has few points of connection with her mother and her mother's life choices. "She was a housewife and didn't understand the whole education thing. I used to like to go hunting and fishing with my dad, to hang out with him and talk to him. She hated that. She always said, 'Go ask your dad; he is the smart one around here. He's the one who's buying you the BMW!' "

Many girls discover that when alone with their fathers, they were able to connect on a different and deeper level and discover their father's capacity to love them. Even in small doses, this kind of nurturing made a difference.

What About the Brothers?

Boys seem to have a different kind of relationship with Mother. Just about every daughter of a narcissistic mother has reported to me that her brother or brothers were better liked and more favored than she or her sisters were. Daughters consistently report how hurtful this has been. Typically, the mother appears not to notice the imbalance, or if confronted, denies it, but it does make some sense. Her sons are not threatening to her in relation to the father as another girl or woman is, because the boys are not as much an extension of her as is a daughter.

An exception to this can occur when the brother gets married and brings a daughter-in-law into the equation, who can begin to feel the brunt of Mother's jealousy. In Mom's eyes, she's a competitor and the two of them may compete for the son's attention. His mother may have been the center of his life before, but his new bride steps into that role. Mother should take a backseat, which is virtually impossible for her. My heart always aches for the wives of men with narcissistic mothers. They don't really know what they are getting into.

- Jillian's brothers got special treatment, and at times it was quite inappropriate. Their mother "was seductive with them. She paraded around the house half-naked and when they were teenagers talked to them about how to be good lovers."

- Lisa had five brothers who could do no wrong in Mother's eyes. "She adored them. They worked on the farm, they bought her gifts, and she worshipped everything they bought for her. They catered to my mother, and she loved that. Even today, they would blame my father for the way Mom acted. They always stuck up for her and she for them. She really brainwashed them! Having sons on a farm was a big plus— girls were not as important. She even went to extremes to keep my brothers out of the service. She would say they were needed on the farm—anything to keep them from leaving. For me, on the other hand, she couldn't wait until I grew up, got married, and moved away."

- Mirabelle's mother wrote a letter to her after visiting her for a few days. "I admire your brother Gerald, as he knows what it's like to know God. Perhaps you'd like to know. And your brother Craig is such a good, hardworking family man. His children are the delight of the family. We always feel welcome in our sons' homes. We don't have to walk on eggshells or worry about what we say. It's always a great time! Coming to your perfect house is such a strain, my dear! I must say that you take after your paternal grandmother. She always thought she was right! You seem to follow her path!" Mirabelle brought this letter to therapy. She was wondering what it all meant. "Why are my brothers favored so? What have I done wrong? What does she mean, 'your perfect house'? Is she jealous of me? Why is she saying I take after the grandmother whom I detested and so did she? She is so hateful! God, it hurts! She doesn't like my sister either. She recently started a letter to my sister with, 'Dear Mandy . . . I only say "dear" because I carried you in my womb.' "

- Amelia had one brother who was the king to their mother. "He was two years older than I, and he was put on a pedestal—the trophy boy. Mom related to him and wanted attention from him. A lot of her energy went to him. In adulthood it became crazier, and he became really rich. If my sisters or I would invite her over, she would dump us if my brother had invited her over too."

- For many, the playing field between brothers and sisters has never been level. Victoria reports, "My brother is 18 now. I basically raised him and I really love him. He calls me when he is in trouble or needs emotional support. But I have to say he got the preferential treatment from Mom. My brother makes C's and she doesn't care. If I made an A minus, it was a big deal. I got a scholarship to law school. It was expected of me. I always had curfews, but my brother did not. He can come in completely drunk and she doesn't care—she'll offer to make him breakfast. My brother got arrested this week outside a bar and she thought it was funny. He can drink and act crazy and she says, 'Boys will be boys.' He dates a Hooters waitress and that is okay, but she hates my medical school boyfriend. My mother constantly defends my brother and criticizes me."

- Every Christmas throughout their childhood, Liz's brother would get twice the number of presents she did. Furthermore, her mother tried to set up competition between the two siblings when the packages were counted. Guess who lost?

It has been surprising to me that most of the daughters I have interviewed or treated have not felt intense resentment toward their brothers. Most of them are grateful that the brothers are getting some maternal attention even if they themselves did not receive it. Some, of course, do feel resentful, and that makes sense. It seems to help the daughter if her brothers can break out of their own denial to see the real problems between their mother and sister. The daughter can then feel some validation from her brother.

- Tara had never gotten a fair shake from either her father or brother. Both of them always blamed Tara for her difficult relationship with her mom. She was 45 years old when her brother finally said to her, "What in the world is wrong with you and Mom and your relationship since like . . . birth?" She had waited a long time, but finally felt validated. "He is now able to see there is a problem, and that means the world to me. It makes me feel less crazy."

The Sisters Extreme

When two daughters are being raised by the same narcissistic mother, I found that, more times than not, they take on very different roles. Both girls internalize the same message that they are valued for what they do, rather than who they are, but they behave in opposite ways. One sister may internalize the message and say, "Okay, I will show you what I can do and how worthy I am" and become an overachiever and a perfectionist. The other sister may internalize this message of inferiority and give up, feeling that she can't make the grade anyway; she becomes an underachiever or engages in some kind of lifelong self-sabotage. We will explore this phenomenon more in Part Two when we discuss life patterns of daughters of narcissistic mothers. The most important part of this to remember is that even though the external landscapes I describe seem like polar opposites, the *internal* landscapes are strikingly similar. In other words, the lifestyles of the women may appear quite different, as the high-achieving daughter will look more successful on the outside, but on the inside, both sisters hear the same negative, internalized messages and struggle emotionally. If there is only one girl in the family, she tends to take one of the polar extremes and become either high-achieving or self-sabotaging.

What causes a daughter to take the high-achieving path versus the self-sabotaging path? I have wondered a lot about this. According to my clinical study, the high-achieving daughter usually had someone special in her life who gave her unconditional love and support, typically the father, an aunt, grandmother, or teacher. The self-sabotaging daughter either had no one to nurture her or had only limited access to an adult who served that role during her childhood.

My sister and I took extreme polar opposite paths, perhaps because, when my sister was very young, we moved away from our grandmother, who was a loving presence for me in my early years, offering encouragement and nurturing. My sister missed this special loving connection with our grandmother and has struggled more in certain areas of her life than I. But we have both definitely fought with the internal critical messages instilled in us.

Daughters of narcissistic mothers seem to relate to extremes in all aspects of their lives and seem overly tolerant of aberrant and unusual behavior, which of course their mothers often exhibited. I even thought at one point that the title of this book might be *Women of Extremes.* A quick overview of what we have learned so far exhibits the extremes that daughters of narcissistic mothers have learned to live with:

- Narcissism itself causes a person to swing from grandiose feelings to deep depression, almost like bipolar disorder.
- As a spectrum disorder, narcissism can range from a few traits to a full-blown narcissistic personality disorder.
- Maternal narcissism takes the extreme of engulfing or ignoring.
- Daughters of narcissistic mothers seem to favor opposite ends of a continuum of life patterns, either success-oriented and high-achieving or self-sabotaging.
- Daughters' relationships with men tend to be either codependent or dependent.

The Shiny Red Apple with the Worm Inside

Narcissistic families are disconnected emotionally. They may appear solid on the exterior, but authentic communication and connections between the members rarely take place because the parents in this family are focused on themselves. They expect the children to react to their needs, instead of the other way around, as in a healthy family. In this dysfunctional system, adults do not deal with real feelings, and therefore do not meet the emotional needs of the children.

In a healthy family, the parents are emotionally connected, happy with each other, in control of the family, and at the top of a hierarchy.[2] Their job is to take care of the children, who look up to them for support and protection. The parents shine love down on the children and strive to meet their needs physically, emotionally, intellectually, and spiritually. A diagram of the healthy family, adapted from a structural family therapy model, looks like this:

Healthy Family Model

Boundary Around Parents' Relationship

Mother and Father Bonded with Each Other

Hierarchy

Children All on Same Level

Needs of Children Being Met

Boundary Around Single Parent

Hierarchy

Children All on Same Level

Needs of Children Being Met

In unhealthy families, this hierarchy becomes skewed, and the children end up taking care of the parents. In a family with a narcissistic mother, everybody attends to the mother, and other family members' needs are not met. In the narcissistic family the mother is at the center of the system with the rest of the family revolving around her, like the planets revolving around the sun, as in this diagram, below:

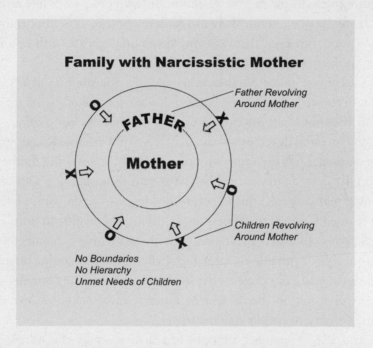

Family with Narcissistic Mother

Father Revolving Around Mother

FATHER

Mother

Children Revolving Around Mother

No Boundaries
No Hierarchy
Unmet Needs of Children

The diagram displays Mother's self-absorption and Father's pact to take care of her. The unspoken rule in these families is that they do not discuss this dynamic and it becomes a family secret. In order to maintain the peace, the children have to keep quiet and not rock the boat. They fear abandonment, which causes them to mask their real feelings and pretend that everything is okay—a survival mechanism. In doing so, they do not learn to express or even be in touch with their feelings, and they are thus set up for many interpersonal difficulties later on in life.

When children can't rely on their parents to meet their needs, they cannot develop a sense of safety, trust, or confidence. Trust is a colossal development issue. Without the learning of trust in our early years, we are set up to have a major handicap with believing in ourselves and feeling safe in intimate connections. Daughters who grew up in narcissistic families uniformly report a lack of confidence in their own decision making as well as difficulty with assuredness in their love relationships. In the recovery section of this book, we will examine what can be done about this void in development. It is important to understand, however, that resolving trust complications will be a lifelong recovery task.

Oftentimes when Mother is narcissistic, she may be able to do some of the earlier nurturing because she has control of the infant and small child and can mold the child to her wishes. But as the child grows older and develops a mind of her own, the mother loses control and no longer has the same kind of power. This causes the mother to begin her demeaning, critical behavior with the child, in hopes of regaining that control, which is crazy-making for the daughter. Even if she learned a modicum of trust as an infant, she begins to unlearn it as she grows older. As she makes natural, reasonable demands on her mother, who is unable to meet them, the mother becomes resentful and threatened, and projects her inadequacies onto the daughter. She begins to focus on the daughter's failings, rather than on her own limited ability to parent effectively.

You may remember that the characteristics of the narcissistic mother in chapter 1 included a sense of entitlement. This means the narcissist thinks she deserves the best, the most important treatment, being the first in line, being treated with extraordinary efforts, and so on. It also means that her daughter will not be able to have a sense of entitlement, because there is never room for both. Adult feelings of entitlement are unhealthy and dysfunctional, yet as small, helpless, dependent children we are entitled to be cared for. Every child deserves to have someone in her life who is irrationally crazy about her! We gradually grow out of this entitlement and dependency and learn to take care of and rely on ourselves emotionally, which is a sign of stable mental health.

In order to take good care of ourselves as we move through life, girls need to develop sound boundaries between themselves and others. They also need to be able to state what they need in relationships. The daughter of a narcissistic mother does not get to do this, particularly if those needs interfere with what Mother wants. This then causes the daughter to repress her feelings and needs, deny herself, and learn to be fake. Without healthy boundaries, all relationships become skewed in some way.

Setting healthy boundaries requires direct statements and clear communication. Narcissistic families commonly have a skewed, ineffective communication style called "triangulation." Instead of the mother talking to the daughter, the mother may express her thoughts and feelings—usually negative and criticizing—to another family member in the hope that he or she will tell the daughter. Then the mother can deny that she said it, although the message somehow got out there anyway. This triangulation in communication is passive-aggressive and is an expression of the sentiment "I will get you back, but not directly to your face." Many families, unfortunately, communicate in this dysfunctional manner, but narcissistic families are the poster example.

In recovery you will learn to say it like it is. No more pretense, no more facade, no more inauthentic representations of ourselves.

Like a shiny red apple with a worm inside, the narcissistic family hides profound pain. To understand how these relationship dynamics set up the daughter to unconsciously create unhealthy life patterns, we have to discuss further the concern that the narcissistic family has about its image. "It's all about Mom" and "It's all about image" are its mottoes.

CHAPTER FIVE

IMAGE IS EVERYTHING:
PUT A SMILE ON THAT PRETTY LITTLE FACE

Image! Image was all that mattered to Mom. She was obsessed with appearance right up until she died at age fifty-
four from complications during a liposuction.
—Joanie, 45

P ut a smile on that pretty little face. Throw back your shoulders,
hold up your head, and don't let the world know that you are
unhappy." As a child, I was told this repeatedly. I cannot count the
times I felt like frowning or crying and my mother would cite those
lines to me. It hurts to smile if the feeling underneath is sadness, anger,
confusion, or some other kind of pain. Sometimes it just feels good to
frown, be sad, be angry—in other words, *be real.*

How It Looks Is More Important
Than How It Feels

Daughters of narcissistic mothers are told plainly in words or by their
mothers' example: *"How you look is more important than who you
are or how you feel."* The "image message" has little to do with
healthy selfhood; it springs from the internal insecurity and fragile
ego of the narcissistic mother. Narcissists typically put on a great
show so that others think they are special or unique, and they even

convince themselves of this. But at their core is a disoriented, ill-developed sense of self that is very small, incomplete, and defective.

Our culture's materialism, advanced technology, and material wealth reinforce the importance of image and presentation for everyone. But women are subjected to it more constantly and are more vulnerable to persistent cultural ideals of thinness, fitness, and perfection. Daughters of narcissistic mothers are not only pressured by the culture, they're also pressured by their mothers' ceaseless messages about maintaining a perfect image. For us, it is a double whammy! These combined forces present a tremendous challenge for the girl or woman trying to be her own person. Below we will discuss the image messages we got from Mother and then see how our narcissistic culture frosts the cake with lavish reinforcement.

Projecting the "Right" Image: Maternal Reflections

In *Postcards from the Edge,* the movie based on Carrie Fisher's semi-autobiographical novel, the mother (Shirley MacLaine) is ill and in the hospital. All she worries about is her hair and makeup, and she tells her daughter that she does not want to be buried without her eyebrows. Her daughter (Meryl Streep) explains the family to a doctor this way: "We're designed more for public than for private."[1] The women I've treated and interviewed agree.

Image is what Mother wants the world to see about *her,* and she expects her daughter to polish that image further, and carry it for the family into the world. But most daughters are overpowered by this expectation. They can't carry their mothers' image and they have trouble establishing their own.

- Tonya, 28, confides, "Mom so wanted me to be the 'image girl.' She wanted the most popular girl in school, dating the football player, majorette and prom queen type. I was not that kind of teenager and it was a big disappointment to her. I had anxiety disorders and low self-esteem."

Daughters internalize maternal messages about image that can persist well into their lives as independent adults. Bella said, "I learned that it is about how it looks, not how it feels. I picked this up in my personal appearance and my home. I wish I didn't do this, but it doesn't matter who is coming over to my house, I want it to look pretty. Our house with Mom was always pretty and clean. I don't walk around without makeup on, except when alone with my husband. I like to take care of myself, and I am very competitive with other women if we go out. I feel pressure from society to be thin, pretty, and look nice."

- "This image thing was a strong message," says Jessica, 43. "To this day, I keep things looking good and hunky-dory at my house. No one in our family knows that my husband and I have any problems. It made me concerned about how I look too. Now I want to have a boob job and I am jealous of other women."

- "When my mother died, she was in a coma for a time," recalls Magda, 55. "The nurses had pulled her hair back in a braid, and it looked awful. When she died and I went over to the mortuary and saw her body, she still had this stupid braid. My dad had dressed her appropriately, but that braid! All I could think of was she wouldn't be caught dead with her hair like that!"

- Living up to Mother's expectations sometimes requires surrendering personal choice. Charlie told me, "My mother put special efforts into how my sister and I looked. We were always perfectly matched with bows, colors, shoes, and outfits. I don't remember choosing something that I wore until I was at least 14."

Mother sometimes completely disregards a girl's wishes, and the daughter may end up feeling that she is an object, not a person. My own mother used to braid my hair so tightly my eyes would slant and I would cry and say it hurt. Her message back was, "It hurts to be beautiful!" I still don't know what that really means. Does it mean that if I don't look a certain way, I won't be successful, accepted, or loved? And that to look the accepted way, it has to hurt? What a disturbing worldview that was! The endless focus on beauty can become exhausting.

- Trisha, 34, says, "There was always the 'looks' issue. My mother would always pull my bangs off my face and say, 'Look at her face.' I got kicked out of the house when I was 13 because my bangs were too long. Mother just walked up to me one day and cut them off."

- Sonja's mother used to recite, "We must, we must, we must improve our bust," and tell her, "Good God, girl, do those exercises. Don't you know that no man will even notice you if you don't develop bosoms?"

An obsession with "how things look" can cause the narcissistic mother (or grandmother) to neglect basic parenting responsibilities. Amanda tells about the time that her daughter got in serious trouble with the law and had to go to court. Local journalists took a strong interest in the case, and there were reporters everywhere. Amanda needed her mother's support, but her mother was too concerned about image to show up: "She said she couldn't go to court with me and her granddaughter because she couldn't handle the media seeing her break down. Mom carried on about how my kids are always in trouble and how she didn't raise her kids to be like this. As if it was about her! It's always too much for her to handle!" Amanda got some spunk when she finally told her mother, "Ya know, Mom, I like my kids better than I like yours!"

- Cassie got to the point in her young adulthood where she wouldn't tell her mother anything because her mother used it as a tool either to prove how wonderful or how stupid Cassie was, depending on how it made her mother look. "She always wanted me to marry a doctor. She used my accomplishments like a badge. She would set me up with sleazy doctors to date and then scan me to see if I looked okay. Was I presentable? Did I embarrass her?"

- Leslie, 58, remembers as a child worrying about her parents' financial situation. "They must have talked about it in front of me. I decided I needed to help. Codependent-trained me. So I called my grandmother and asked her if she would please send some money to my poor parents to help them. Reasonable, huh? Well, grandmother dear had a bit of narcissism as well. The next time she saw me, she raked me over the coals. 'Don't ever call me and say anything personal again, especially about money and your parents! We have a party line out here in the country and the neighbors can hear!' Well, let's see, I think I was about seven years old at the time. Tell you something? Yes, Granny, I won't embarrass you again. Forget about what I was feeling as a little girl worrying about her parents. I wonder, did I think then, What about me? Probably not, I must have felt just like a bad kid who had done something wrong— again."

- If a daughter doesn't fulfill her mother's goals for her, sometimes the daughter is made to feel as if her true accomplishments don't matter. Julie, 30, remembers,

"Whenever I was getting ready to go to my middle school Open House Night with my parents, Mom tortured me about what I was going to wear and how I would wear my hair. She never said anything about my project being chosen as one of the best in the class. Never took the time to look through my folders in each of my classrooms. I never got the feeling that Mom valued the things I valued about myself."

• The relentless focus on image leaves no room for true feelings. Often, the daughter is forced to be insincere to fit the mother's image. Maya, 22, told me, "After Mom and Dad split up, Mom always instructed me to appear happy whenever I was with Dad. 'Don't show him that we are suffering without him,' she'd tell me. I was suffering, but I did not want to disobey her, so I felt as if I was literally pasting a fake smile on my face. And when Dad would ask how I was doing, I'd say, 'Great. Everything's going fine!' Lying like that made me feel guilty, like I was betraying my father."

Because we internalize these kinds of messages throughout our childhood and adolescence, we ourselves become image-focused. We feel like we never measure up. And the narcissistic culture in which we live powerfully reinforces these childhood messages.

Projecting the "Right" Image: Cultural Reflections

American culture today in general maintains an image founded on "what" instead of on "who." Messages to perform, excel, and be beautiful bombard every aspect of daily life, and the general incidence of narcissism appears to be rising. As Alexander Lowen cites in his book *Narcissism: Denial of the True Self*:

When wealth occupies a higher position than wisdom, when notoriety is admired more than dignity, when success is more important than self-respect, the culture itself overvalues "image" and must be regarded as narcissistic.[2]

The strivings of today's youth say it all too clearly. A *USA Today* article on Generation Y (ages 18–25) states their greatest life goals are to become rich and famous:

> When you open a celebrity magazine, it's all about the money and being rich and famous . . . anything from *The Apprentice,* where the intro to the show is the "money song" to *US Weekly* magazine, where you see all the celebrities and their six-million-dollar homes. We see reality TV shows with Jessica and Nick living the life. We see Britney and Paris. The people we relate to outside our friends are those people.[3]

An exposé or a documentary could be made about the media influence on narcissism, especially that of reality television—*Dr. 90210, Drastic Plastic Surgery, It's Good to Be, MTV Cribs,* and *Extreme Makeover*—to name a few. A particularly sad example jumped out at me on a show called *Body Work* that I recently viewed on TLC.

A young girl, maybe sixteen years old, was going to a plastic surgeon for a nose job. Her mother had undergone some previous surgeries and Botox treatments from the same doctor. The doctor tells the young girl that she is pretty. She tells him that she may be pretty, but not compared to the other girls at her school. She attends a private school and goes on to say that at her school, nothing but perfection is acceptable.

Do we want our children to think like this? Do we want our children to be a reflection of this kind of "glitter mentality"? According to a nationwide study conducted for Girls Inc. called *The Supergirl Dilemma,* girls as young as ten feel "a lot of pressure to be athletic, pretty, and skinny plus smart."[4] Almost every women's magazine on the newsstand is packed with articles on how to look better, how to attract and keep an eligible man, how to be a career success, even how to raise successful children. But beauty continues to serve as the bedrock. According to *The Supergirl Dilemma,* "The findings point to the expectations . . . that a girl's appearance is still her most important asset." [5]

As Audrey Brashich writes in *All Made Up:*

Fifty-nine percent of teen girls are reportedly dissatisfied with their body shape, 66 percent desire to lose weight, and over half report that the appearance of models in the magazines influences their image of a perfect female body. And some girls are more afraid of becoming fat than they are of nuclear war, cancer, or losing their parents. [6]

The images seen in entertainment, on fashion runways, on television, in magazines, and in the media in general undeniably affect how women feel about themselves. The daughter of a narcissistic mother has to deal with this rampant media obsession with image as well as the warped maternal counsel that appearance is everything.

Female respondents in a survey done recently by Dove Corporation said that they felt pressure to try to be the "perfect" picture of beauty as depicted by advertisers in our culture:

[Sixty-three percent] strongly agree that women today are expected to be more attractive than their mother's generation. [Sixty percent] strongly agree that society expects women to enhance their physical attractiveness. [Forty-five percent] of women feel women who are more beautiful have greater opportunities in life. And more than half strongly agree that physically attractive women are more valued by men. More than two-thirds (68%) of women strongly agree that the media and advertising set an unrealistic standard of beauty that most women can't ever achieve. Well over half of all women (57%) strongly agree that the attributes of female beauty have become very narrowly defined in today's world. [7]

According to the Dove study, only 2 percent of women describe themselves as beautiful and only 13 percent are satisfied with their body weight and shape. I have been quite impressed with the Dove gals who allowed themselves to be photographed in their underwear and even in some nude shots, and who seem to be breaking free from the cultural yoke of perfectionism. Yet thousands of other women will spend $5,000 to $6,000 to have the flab on their arms removed.[8] Less invasive methods of retouching can be used with a camera made by Hewlett-Packard called Photosmart R-927, which has a slimming feature that digitally removes those ten pounds a camera supposedly tacks on.[9]

In some middle- and upper-middle-class families, it was customary for a girl to receive a car for her sixteenth birthday. Now, in many circles, the coming-of-age gift is a breast implant.

Since some people are willing to pay the big bucks for "the look," plastic surgery is exploding. Between 1997 and 2003, the number of cosmetic procedures in America increased by over 220 percent, and teens are increasingly being given breast augmentation as graduation gifts. In one year, the number of girls eighteen and younger getting breast implants jumped nearly threefold, from 3,872 in 2002 to 11,326 in 2003.[10]

I started trying to offset the media assault for my own daughter when she was only five years old by telling her, "It's what's on the inside that counts." One day, she and her five-year-old playmate were standing in front of a mirror primping and looking at their hair. Her little friend said, "Aren't we pretty, Meggan?" My well-informed but too-young-to-understand daughter told her playmate, "My mommy says that it is nice that we are pretty, but it's our guts and our veins that are really important!" Okay, perhaps I started a little early, but I was trying to give her an important message for the future.

Authentic Reflections

A young girl absorbs how to be a woman, wife, lover, friend, and mother from both her mother and her culture. When a healthy, secure mother assists her daughter in managing the cultural onslaught of image messages about celebrity, wealth, and perfect beauty, the daughter gets the correct message that healthy womanhood is about who she is—her value system, standards, courage, integrity, inner fortitude, capacity for love and empathy and her personal mode of conduct. But women who were taught that how they appear is more important than personal feelings, identity, values, and authenticity feel empty. Whenever I heard Tina Turner sing "What's Love Got to Do with It?" I really wished that the message were "What's *Beauty* Got to Do with It?" Love actually has everything to do with our healthy development.

In order to recover from this emptiness and image-oriented life view, the daughter of a narcissistic mother first has to learn how to tune in to who she is as a person. She begins sorting out the things that make her beautiful and unique and separating herself from the inauthentic, automatic reactions to people and her environment to which she has become accustomed. Before we begin these important steps of recovery, however, I want you to see how your childhood with a narcissistic mother has affected your decisions about career, relationships, parenting, and your place in the world. Join me, and together we will see some distinct patterns.

PART TWO

How Narcissistic Mothering Affects Your Entire Life

In the previous section we laid out the characteristics and dynamics of maternal narcissism. Now we will look at how these dynamics directly affect your life.

Daughters of narcissistic mothers absorb the message "I am valued for what I do, rather than for who I am." As we mature, this potent credo can make us act in two wildly different ways: as high achievers and as self-saboteurs.

Being raised by a narcissistic mother has far-reaching effects that brand your soul. To excise this brand and become your own person, you will need to work through the recovery program in part 3. But first you need to identify which behavior pattern is yours.

CHAPTER SIX

I Try So Hard!

THE HIGH-ACHIEVING DAUGHTER

I decided early on, like at age ten, that working hard was
the only way to feel good about myself, and to compensate
for all the "not good enough" messages. I wish someone
had told me it wouldn't fill the bill as I imagined it would.
The hard-work escape sounded good at the time.
—Kerry, 35

The high-achieving daughter, whom I call Mary Marvel,[1] em-
barks on a whirlwind of achievement, out to prove to her
mother and to the world just how good she can be. "I am worthy,"
she is trying to tell herself and her mother, "because of the extraordi-
narily impressive things I can accomplish." She finds it difficult to
love herself just for who she is. She bases her worth on her accomplishment and her busyness. When not accomplishing something
she (or others) thinks is great, she feels worthless. The high achiever
becomes a "human doing" rather than a "human being" who is accepted for and comfortable just being herself.

Such women appear to be superheroes, but their productivity and
achievement don't make them feel accomplished or comfortable on
the inside. They never give themselves the credit they deserve and
continually struggle with feelings of inadequacy. Constantly looking
for more things they can do to prove themselves, they are often chron-

ically exhausted, unaware of how this drive to achieve inhibits their ability to take care of themselves. Mary Marvels can be highly educated and professional or stay-at-home, perfectionist homemakers, but they feel nothing they do is ever good enough.

Are you a Mary Marvel? One way to identify whether you are is to look at how you define yourself. Do you typically describe yourself as who you are: "I am a loving, kind person who strives to be honest and to live a life that contributes to society in some significant way"? Or is your identity more closely tied to what you do: "I am a CEO for a large manufacturing firm, I am a business owner, I am an attorney, or I am a mother of four and a Girl Scout leader who also teaches Sunday school"?

You might have learned that you had to be a doer for your mother in order to be accepted or approved. If your mother was an "accomplishment-oriented" narcissist, as discussed in chapter 3, you grew up emulating this role model and following the rule that you had to "achieve to be worthy." Even though this was expected of you, however, your accomplishments don't really make you feel good about yourself. For no matter how much you try to accomplish and perform, you still hear the internal message: It's not enough.

This attitude is frustrating, sad, and difficult. There is always a push to do more, but doing more makes you feel better about yourself only temporarily. So you up the ante, hoping somehow that it *will* work in the end. Most daughters of narcissistic mothers don't understand the origins of this impulse, but feel they need to keep it up. As Pressman and Pressman say in their book, *The Narcissistic Family*, "The roots of workaholism are truly sown in narcissistic homes; 'I do, therefore I am' could be the motto of many adult children from these homes."[2]

- Rosa is a pretty but harried-looking woman who is constantly doing more than her fair share of work within any group. She explains, "I have to work so hard to justify just being here—have to do and do and do."

- Mother of three and a college professor, Jerilyn started on her path during the early years. She relates, "I've been doing this race for the good since I was a kid. Straight A's, AP classes in high school, every sport offered, in all the music programs, honors programs, straight to college and then on to grad school. It all looks great, but somehow it feels like I am trying to prove something to justify my existence."

I have to admit this category fits me. Sometimes I have been able to give myself credit for what I have accomplished, but even when I've done so, I still feel something might be missing. Throughout my life, it would actually make me angry when others asked why I was doing something more— another degree, another business idea, another major project. You yourself probably won't really be able to explain it to yourself until you complete recovery and uncover all the dynamics behind it. We daughters may try to explain ourselves as being type A personalities, or just overly ambitious. But inside, we know that our personal rat race has another cause. A recurring dream I had in my early years before graduate school illustrates this unconscious compulsion always to work harder and get it right:

I am standing in front of a mirror in the bedroom trying to get dressed. As I am trying on several different outfits in arduous, frustrating slow motion, nothing looks right or is working correctly. I keep changing clothes, regardless. A voice in the hall outside the bedroom is calling me: "Come on, you're okay just the way you are."

I misinterpreted this dream for years, thinking it had something to do with my husband's impatience with me when we were getting ready to go somewhere. I ultimately realized, however, that the voice in the hall was my intuition calling to me, voicing the validation that I am okay as I am.

So, What Does This Mean?

If you fit the description of a Mary Marvel, you may be asking the question "But what if my choices are mine and I am doing what I want, although it just happens to be a higher level of achievement than many people care to pursue? Is this wrong?" Of course, a significant number of high achievers *are* doing things they really want to do. Many daughters of narcissistic mothers who took the Mary Marvel route are truly accomplished, amazing women, and I honor their multitude of talents. In fact, sometimes the narcissistic mother's legacy ends up being a gift that provides you with an inner drive that others may not have. One woman, an exceptionally talented artist, explained it this way:

> I've always felt that my art was something "untouchable"; my narcissistic mother could not affect it because it was an inner event and therefore not subject to her influence. It was a private joy that flourished and thrived as I grew. I had to spend so much time on the inside of myself, not disturbing her, being quiet and unseen, that my drawing abilities sort of became a natural outgrowth of that. If I had to come up with a positive result of growing up in a narcissistic home, that would top my list.

If you are a high achiever pursuing your chosen life dreams, *and* you are giving yourself credit and taking good care of yourself in the process, you are doing it *so* right. High achievement becomes a problem only when you:

- Have medical or mental health problems associated with not taking care of yourself.
- Seek only external validation to define your self-worth.
- Find that you cannot give yourself credit for what you accomplish in all aspects of your life.

Let's look at each of these Mary Marvel pitfalls so that you can make sure they have not entrapped you or, if they have, so that you can take steps to climb out of them.

Lack of Self-Care

Busyness or workaholism can be a form of self-destructive behavior similar to alcoholism and drug or food addiction. It works the same to numb the pain. If you become chronically exhausted, and find that you can't slow down, and are beginning to have health problems, it is time to take an inventory of whether or not your activities fit your own value system (rather than your mother's or your internalized critic) and whether they are healthy for you. Looking strong and invulnerable on the outside may be an attempt to escape the emptiness and pain of feelings of unworthiness on the inside. Here are some women who have begun to come to terms with this behavior:

- Summer feels valued for what she does rather than who she is. "I'm a workhorse. I'm like this because my mother trained me to be. I don't know how to stop. It's affecting my health. I have MS, nine breast biopsies in the past few months, irritable bowel syndrome, can't keep weight on, and arthritis. I work full time, have a side business of four accounting clients, am a Girl Scout troop leader for my daughters, youth athletic coach, make jewelry, and can vegetables. Everybody looks at me for what I do, not realizing there is a *me* inside of there too. I can't sit down. It feels like I am leaping small buildings in a single bound and if I sit down, I will crash."

- Bernie looks at her overachieving with some regret. "I never called in sick at work even when I felt awful. Every job I had, I gave 100 percent. In fact, anything I do gets 100 percent. This is all that makes me good enough. Raising my daughters, sometimes I gave too much to my job when I should have been home with them. I have some regrets about this now, as well as a new diagnosis of fibromyalgia."

- Marlo, 45, tells me, "I am an overachiever, a perfectionist type A with my job, with keeping a meticulous house, with constantly having new goals that I want to obtain. I never feel it is good enough and always that I have to do more. I have constant feelings of anxiety, worry, and excessive stress."

Once you recognize that you are trying to patch up your vulnerability with various modes of achievement, you will see that you have been shortchanging yourself and those you love. Then you'll be able to take steps to change.

Internal Versus External Validation

The need for validation can be a catch-22. If a child did not receive validation in her early developmental years, and as a young woman is not able to validate herself, she often succumbs to the lure of doing more and trying harder in ways that bring validation from others. This is an unconscious seduction because Mary Marvels are almost always highly skilled and competent. It is therefore not difficult to obtain external validation from friends, family, work, or society in general. The praise appears to fill the emptiness, but relying on external praise can create anxiety. Because it is *external* validation, the daughter does not own it or control it and it can be taken away from her at any time. If she does not continue to accomplish, it will also disappear.

When you learn to rely on yourself for validation, on the other hand, you rest peacefully at night. You will be learning more about how to do this in the recovery section of the book, but let's look closely now at why you find it so difficult to give yourself credit.

Am I Arrogant?

Many daughters are afraid to give themselves credit. On the rare occasions when they do, they feel as if they are behaving like a narcissist or at the very least, acting arrogant, like their mothers. If you are worried about emulating your mother in this way, remind yourself that the true narcissist has "a grandiose sense of self-importance, e.g., exaggerates achievements and talents, expects to be recognized as superior without commensurate achievements."[3]

The narcissist is arrogant in disingenuous ways, and most times with nothing to back up the bragging spree. She needs to make herself look bigger than she really is because she feels inadequate. But most high-achieving, Mary Marvel daughters have a ton of very real achievements because they have worked so hard. It is not narcissistic to be proud of your achievements and accomplishments. You do not need to brag, but give *yourself* the credit you deserve. By giving yourself credit where credit is due, you can help slow down the rat race of do, do, do. Feel good about what you have already done.

Am I an Impostor?

Another reason high-achieving Mary Marvels have difficulty giving themselves internal praise is a fear called the "impostor syndrome." Someone who suffers from the impostor syndrome is unable to accept and claim her accomplishments, no matter what level of success she has achieved or maintained. She may have abundant proof of her hard-won accomplishments, including wealth and material goods, but remains convinced that she either doesn't deserve her success or that she is just a fraud. She dismisses outward signs of accomplishments as just luck or good timing. An "impostor" usually feels as if she has been deceptive, having made others think she is more intelligent or skilled than she believes herself to be. Most people who admit to feeling like impostors are women, although there is some evidence that many men feel this way too.

High-achieving daughters of narcissistic mothers are at great risk for the impostor syndrome because we were raised to feel we were never good enough. When a woman does not feel worthy internally, she believes that she is undeserving and cannot accept success or recognition.

- Lonnie, 46, a very bright, accomplished owner of her own clothing company, puts it this way: "I have a knack for appearing competent when I don't think I really am. I'm always worried that someone will find out that I'm not really very good at my job. I just know how to put on a good show. This bothers me and I know someday someone will find this out and call me a fake."

- Ellen, 57, a successful real estate agent, does not attribute her success to her own efforts: "Every time I make a big sale, even though I know I worked my butt off, I regard it as luck or just a fluke that the money came my way once again and predict that the next time will be a failure."

- Karena, 38, recalls how she felt right after receiving her Ph.D.: "I actually wrote that damn dissertation, but believe me, I won't ever let anyone read it. I don't want anyone to see how dumb it sounds. It is amazing I got that degree. Maybe my field is a particularly easy one or the professors felt they had to pass me after all this time."

In the above examples, you see how women discount their real successes. In addition to these tendencies, high-achieving daughters tend to disparage themselves and play down their positive attributes because they fear that someone will find them arrogant. This behavior is a holdover from growing up as the target of Mother's envy.

An article titled "Introduction of the Impostor Syndrome" details some narcissistic family dynamics.

Attitudes, beliefs, direct or indirect messages that we received from our parents or from other significant people in our lives early on may have contributed to the development of impostor feelings. Certain family situations and dynamics tend to contribute to impostor feelings: when the success and career aspirations conflict with the family expectations of the gender, race, religion, or age of the person, families who impose unrealistic standards, families who are very critical, and families who are ridden with conflict and anger.[4]

High-achieving daughters with the impostor syndrome are at great risk for "generalized anxiety, lack of self-confidence, depression, and frustration related to inability to meet self-imposed standards of achievement,"[5] and cannot usually stop proving their worth until they work through a recovery program.

Even after extended and repeated experiences of success, the impostor feeling does not appear to lessen. This is the lasting power of internalized messages. Incredibly competent women share the following stories:

- Lillian wants to relax and rest on her laurels, but cannot. "I could never measure up as a kid. If I brought home a B, it was always 'Where's the A?' If I cleaned the bathroom, I had to redo it because it wasn't clean enough. Now as an adult, I am a successful screenwriter and should be able to finally feel some success, but I never give myself credit because I never know when the next shoe will drop. Something could happen that would make my proud self sit in shame once again."

- Cassidy always questions herself: "I went to medical school and did very well. I have found deep passion in helping other people and love my job. People call me 'Doctor' and look up to me and ask for my help and advice. Even though I can see

I have these important skills now, I wonder if I dare allow myself credit for all this hard work. I am a high achiever and always have been, but Mother always warned me, 'Don't get a big head.' "

- Lela, 59, makes certain that she takes care of herself, but though "I feel good enough at times, it never lasts long. My self-esteem can get shattered easily. Self-doubt is but a thought away. My husband often says to me, 'Do you have any idea how awesome you are?' I am truly astounded that I get awards. Why would they pick me? My résumé is about six pages long, but I can't even say 'You go, girl' to myself."

- Jeanie, 45, reports, "The odds were stacked against me. I had no support at home. I got validation at school. I would enter speech contests, I played sports, I was valedictorian. But inside I cried myself to sleep at night. From age 14 to 20, I was clinically depressed and didn't know it. School was my outlet. That is where people would say I was smart and okay. I would accept my awards with my head down and hunched over. I covered myself with a lot of clothes in my teens. I had a nice figure, but I wanted to hide from people. No confidence really. I was so modest. I could not strut my stuff or Mother would have emotionally abused me. I still underplay myself to others. No one gave me any guidance. In business, I managed to go from nothing to making it in the corporate world. With no insight in how to do it, I am in public relations and a seasoned professional now. I know I have worked hard, but I always feel like a fraud, an impostor. Putting myself down. It is an exhausting way to live."

The narcissistic mothers of these talented, seasoned, even wise and self-aware women hijacked their young accomplishments. But now they continue to do this to themselves. I find comfort and inspiration in this favorite passage by Marianne Williamson, and hope you will too. And I hope you will start the recovery process in part 3.

> Our deepest fear is not that we are inadequate. Our deepest fear is that we are powerful beyond measure. It is our light, not our darkness that most frightens us. We ask ourselves, who am I to be brilliant, gorgeous, talented, fabulous? Actually, who are you not to be? You are a child of God. Your playing small does not serve the world. There is nothing enlightened about shrinking so that other people won't feel insecure around you. We are all meant to shine, as children do. We were born to make manifest the glory of God that is within us. It's not just in some of us; it's in everyone. And as we let our own light shine, we unconsciously give other people permission to do the same. As we are liberated from our own fear, our presence automatically liberates others.[6]

Does the Glass Slipper Fit?

If you find you fit the description of Mary Marvel, know you are not alone. Your path to recovery will become clear in part 3 of this book. Many daughters of narcissistic mothers got the message to do well—but not too well, because they might outshine Mom. I don't want to give you a mixed message too, so let me say again that your accomplishments are truly a marvel. You have overcome great odds and are an amazing woman and now you need to care for yourself and give yourself the credit you deserve. Then you will be able to enjoy the marvel that you truly are and cherish yourself as you deserve.

CHAPTER SEVEN

What's the Use?

THE SELF-SABOTAGING DAUGHTER

> Chrissie too saw the advantages of the hard-work escape
> route, but did not take it. There was a perverse, wicked,
> rebellious streak in Chrissie, which has led her to a kind
> of liberation. She was a shrewd little thing, and she had
> seen what was happening. What good did it do you to
> work so hard, to pass your exams, to go to university like
> a good girl? You ended up miserable, cooped up, trapped
> just the same.
> —Margaret Drabble, *The Peppered Moth*[1]

All daughters of narcissistic mothers to some extent give up along the way. For each one of us was but a child, not a seasoned warrior, when we had to begin to fight battle after battle for our own identity. Not one of us has been able to fulfill our mother's expectations. Those of us who did not become overachievers to prove our mothers wrong chose the polar opposite route and took our anger out on ourselves, unwittingly sabotaging our own efforts. Feeling angry at Mother for creating a no-win situation in which she will never approve of us, in effect we say to Mother, "See? I'm proving that I can't be who you want me to be!"

The self-saboteur is the high achiever's internal twin. Although they've taken different paths and created contrasting lifestyles, their internal landscapes and emotional issues are the same.

Are you a self-saboteur? Some of the traits include:

1. Giving up
2. Numbing the pain with various addictions
3. Staying stuck in self-destructive lifestyles
4. Underachievement

Here are some stories of self-sabotaging daughters of narcissistic mothers:

- Taryn always plays it safe. Rarely can she point out an instance in her adult life where she took risks for what she wanted. "I am an underachiever because of the 'never feel good enough' message. The fear of failure keeps me from doing the absolute best. If I keep on the middle road, I don't have to deal with failure. I have big ideas and aspirations, but they are dreams rather than goals. I think, Oh, that would be nice to do, but I don't do it. Maybe I wouldn't be good at it."

- Sandra readily describes herself as an underachiever. "I don't feel the need to be great at anything I do. I was never good enough anyway, so why bother trying? I bought a flower shop at age 50, but I never really worked hard at it to make it successful. I never strived to be competitive in work. Just get the job done."

- Sally always has an excuse for missing every opportunity, and says, "I tend not to get involved. I shy away from things. I am very smart, but not confident. I could have done more, but I was afraid and I was not encouraged. The main message I got was just to get married, and that's what I did."

Why do some daughters become high achievers and some self-saboteurs? I have found that, most times, the high achievers had someone special in their lives, a grandmother, aunt, father, or close relative who gave them positive messages to offset or confront the negative ones from their mothers. Many times this special person was loving, and empathetic, and nurturing. The self-saboteur often did not have someone like this to help her or, if she did, did not have him or her long enough to make a difference.

Why Self-Sabotage?

The self-saboteur's patterns and emotional problems are usually a survival response to her unhealthy upbringing. Rarely does any one of us make a conscious choice to be self-destructive. If, however, a child lacks maternal support and nurturing, she will most likely have difficulty understanding and processing her feelings. If your mother denied her own feelings, then she would not have allowed you to have any of your own either.

Young children believe that Mother is the true source and has all the answers. If a mother dislikes her child, or thinks she's not good enough, the child believes she's unlikable and inadequate. If someone does not challenge this distortion and show the child that she is worthy and precious, she will internalize these negative beliefs and eventually decide that she cannot be different.

Let Me Numb My Pain

Left with buried and unprocessed feelings, the daughter begins to find defense mechanisms to cope with her unhappiness, sadness, and emptiness. She may become severely depressed or develop eating disorders, addictions to drugs or alcohol to attempt to self-medicate the pain and inadequacy she feels, or other emotional disorders that disguise or divert attention from the origin of her misery. This becomes a vicious cycle that keeps her numb and immobile. She maintains her inability to accomplish healthy things for herself and in turn reinforces her feelings of worthlessness. She pushes people away with destructive behaviors, which leaves her lonely and empty.

- Sherri's behavior escalated over a period of several years. "I was into sabotaging my life. Lots of sex, looking for love. Started to drink alcohol in high school. I even became a kleptomaniac a couple of years ago, a great escape that went on for about a year. It was like drinking, except the focus was on stealing. I could get away from the pain. But such shame! I had turned on myself."

- Unable to motivate herself to make changes in her life, Meredith, 28, is a classic example of low self-esteem. She went to college but didn't apply herself, and eventually dropped out. She is aware of how she is hurting herself but can still accurately predict, "If I try to do something important, I tend to have severe panic attacks."

- Athena and her sisters all have eating disorders. "My older sister is anorexic and I am bulimic. Another sister is both! We were all hospitalized for the eating disorders and had to have sessions with Mother. She always blamed it on the media, but she constantly puts people down who don't look perfect. She says awful things like, 'How can that woman eat like that? She eats like a pig. And look at that woman's hair!' At the beach she would make comments on people's bodies and their cellulite. I am overweight now and probably always will be. I have given up."

- Nelly, 35, tells me, "Since I was little, I always thought there was something wrong with me. I went through long periods of depression and was even hospitalized for it. Many times, just making it through the day was my goal. I often wanted to

find the highest building and, you know, take a flying leap.
I eventually figured out that I couldn't get angry or have
feelings. I numbed everything, good and bad. When I realized
that something was wrong with how I was raised, I began to
make some big changes."

- Gail, having lived for years in a state of denial, just recently
leveled with herself about what her life has become: "I'm a
flippin' alcoholic. So was Mom, and I swore I'd never be like
her! The worst part of this is how destructive it is to my life.
I can have great things happen and right before I reap the
reward, I go get drunk and mess it all up. It is like I sabotage
everything good, and I get nowhere!"

- Never able to measure up to what her mother wanted,
MariAnn got into drugs early in her teen years and at age
26 is still fighting the addiction. "It has caused me a life of
disaster," she reflects. "I used to work for a doctor's office
and got in trouble for taking prescription pain medicine out
of their cabinets. I thought it was cool until I got caught
and was actually charged with a crime. I go to Narcotics
Anonymous now and have become sober, but it took me a
long time to realize that I was sabotaging everything good
in my life. It makes me so sad to think about all the years
I wasted."

- Damaris is coming to terms with some painful truths.
"Feeling unlovable has some devastating effects. I am
always feeling like I will be rejected or not accepted, so
I find I cannot be assertive with anyone. I just learned in
therapy that I am passive and don't stick up for myself.
This passivity has cost me jobs, relationships, and even a
baby that I gave up for adoption when I didn't want to.
It all makes me cry."

- Candy has been working extremely hard in therapy to release herself from her mother's legacy. "The irony of it all is that I don't feel like I can start living until my mother is deceased. I call it ironic because she brought me into this world. I feel like I am connected to a ball and chain. My struggle for freedom and happiness will only happen when she is gone. Why do I feel like my life will begin when her life ends?"

- Christy tells me, "I was diagnosed as being clinically depressed two years ago and was floored by that reality. I discovered that my family dynamics and my mother's behavior were the root causes. I can also see that my grandmother passed this down to my mom. I have two sisters, and they have both had to deal with their issues with alcoholism and overeating. I am hoping we can all resolve our emptiness inside. I also need help in understanding who I really am and what I want out of life. I am 43 and am still trying to figure out what I want to be when I grow up. I am miserable in my current career."

- Misty frequently uses the word "sabotage" in describing her efforts. She feels that she invalidates virtually every good thing that comes her way. "I know this is a result of something with my mum," she says. "From an early age I'd created a kind of fantasy world in my mind where I was loved and talented because my mother always admired gifted children. Even in my teens, I'd play music and close my eyes and could be anything, usually a great singer, dancer or guitarist, in my mind. At 18, I had a few guitar lessons but was certain I could never be the player of my dreams so gave up. I also enjoyed line dancing until I observed the UK champion; then I thought, Well, what's the point? I can never do anything for the pure fun of it, so end up flitting from one thing to another, getting nowhere. I flounder. Perhaps I am looking for a way to impress my mum before it's too late. I'm not sure what I am looking for or even if I know my 'true self.' "

- Deep down, Janice always wanted to have children. "I always wanted a family. I did marry someone with kids, but never had my own. I get quite sad seeing mums with their children, and I envy their closeness. It is a reminder that my own childhood was stolen from me, and I can never get that back. As a little girl and as a plain child, I was always compared unfavorably to other girls. My mother was a child-minder, and when I was about nine years old there was an incredibly pretty three-year-old girl she looked after. We'd all be out together and Mum would pretend to strangers that this child was hers and that the rest of us were those she minded. She always reminded me that I'd never amount to anything, being no 'oil painting.' Her favorite phrase was, 'When you grow up, I hope you'll have a daughter just like you; then you will know what it's like.' Having my own kids was just too scary. What if I turned out like that?"

As an adult, you *can* loosen the grip of crippling self-doubt and soften the fallout from your mother's lack of love. In fact, you owe it to yourself to address these issues. You do *not* have to resign yourself to self-sabotage. To obstruct or hinder yourself is plain unfair. You are worth so much more. Do not become discouraged, for recovery is possible.

We All Do It

Do not feel alone if this chapter is striking some nerves. All daughters of narcissistic mothers have some self-sabotaging behavior. Although high achievers and self-saboteurs live different lifestyles, both types of daughters engage in self-sabotaging behaviors. Remember: The internal issues of both daughters are the same; they just get played out differently in the external environment. One might be living at the country club and the other on welfare, but both often have issues with depression, anxiety, weight, addictions, health, stress, and relationship problems. Both have internalized the message that they are valued for what they *do*, rather than for who they *are*, and have to resolve the negating internal voices.

Searching for Substitute Caregivers

While it is common to find the high achievers living in nice homes and working in well-paid careers or professions, it is just as common to find the self-saboteurs living in an aunt's basement, in prison, on welfare, and collecting unemployment checks. When children are not allowed to be dependent on their mothers, they search for substitute caretakers as they get older. They attempt to get friends, relatives, lovers, partners, even society to take care of them so that they can finally feel cared for and secure. This may be a way to fool themselves into believing that because they are being cared *for*, they are finally being loved or cared *about*. Yet they never *really* feel cared about.

You can see that this is another method of seeking external validation, just as high achievers seek validation through their accomplishments. But in order to heal and recover, both self-saboteurs and high achievers must find internal validation.

All of the following women are bright, talented, and capable, but not one of them believes in herself. They all report that they have given up, and feel they can't measure up, so why try? They have found alternative methods to keep other people taking care of them in some unhealthy way.

- Peggy was just released from prison for drug possession.
- Sammie is on welfare, a single mother with little money and no car.
- Allie can pay for her apartment, but not food. She gets food stamps and, when starving, collects ketchup packages from

fast-food restaurants to make her own tomato soup with water.

- JoAnn, now 45, still lives in her parents' basement and cannot believe in herself enough to find a job.
- Joelle drinks every day.
- Shelly was just released from the hospital after her boyfriend broke her arm.

Self-sabotaging behavior is not a lack of talent or skill; it is an internal struggle within you. You clearly want to do something, but your internal messages say you cannot or should not. For example, Joelle, above, knows she needs to stay with AA and work on her drinking, but she gets discouraged and drinks anyway. Shelly knows she needs to get out of her bad relationship, but she doesn't want to be alone. JoAnn has a degree in elementary education and could get a job, but feels she won't be accepted so doesn't take the time to fill out the applications. Allie could get a job and have enough food to eat. She just feels too inadequate to try. Peggy knows that drugs are bad for her, but has given up on herself because she feels she will never be loved. Sammie was a straight-A student and honors graduate but keeps getting involved with the wrong men and does not feel good enough about herself to move on. These women desperately want to change, and feel discouraged and trapped. Their internal negative messages are controlling their lives and emotions.

Often the narcissistic mother will be aghast at the self-saboteur's adult life and decide to disown her. Daughters like this cause too much shame and humiliation for a narcissistic mother to handle. What does her child's behavior say about her? What will the neighbors think? What will the relatives think? Of course, any daughter struggling with the above problems would benefit from her mother being there for her emotionally and helping her, but narcissistic mothers tend to worry only about how their daughters' behavior reflects on them and are usually unable to help.

If you are a self-saboteur, it is important to know that you do matter. There are many people who do care about you, and working in recovery will indeed change your life. Your pain and struggle are part of your journey and you had to get to this difficult point to be able to see that you do have what it takes to design your own life and manage your feelings. Regardless of how your mother hurt you, you can heal. I will walk you through the recovery process step by step. Your job is to stay with it and take yourself seriously.

CHAPTER EIGHT

ROMANTIC FALLOUT

TRYING TO WIN AT LOVE
WHERE I FAILED WITH MOM

> If an individual is able to love productively, he loves him-
> self, too; if he can love only others, he cannot love at all.
> —Erich Fromm, *The Art of Loving*[1]

People continue to wonder what love really is. We all pursue it and value it, and each one of us has her own version of how it feels to be in love.

It is common for daughters of narcissistic mothers to try to fill their emotional void and emptiness with inappropriate love rela-tionships. Unfortunately, they often search in all the wrong places for the right partner to validate them. In this chapter, I'll talk about something I call "distorted love." As daughters of narcissistic moth-ers, many of us learn that love means *what someone can do for you or what you can do for them*. Many women unconsciously choose their romantic partners based on this distorted meaning, which sets them up for dependent or codependent relationships—or no rela-tionship at all. The dependent cares about what he can do for you and the codependent cares about what you can do for him. Having no relationship is a kind of giving up, or choosing to not enter the dance at all.

- Alexis, 25, is not sure she knows what to look for as she faces the challenge of searching for a romantic partner. She tells me, "Mom doesn't even use the word 'love' unless she is referring to a pair of shoes! Oh, I guess she does say she loves her cat. How am I supposed to know what love really means?"

Dependent and codependent relationships are not healthy or satisfying connections and many times end up as failed or miserable entanglements. If the relationship ends, the daughter is at risk for repeating the pattern unless she enters recovery and learns to understand that her "relationship picker" has been damaged. The daughter often reenacts her relationship with her mother over and over in what is referred to in psychotherapy circles as "repetition compulsion"—a cycle of relationships that results in disappointment again and again. After their expectations and hopes have been dashed, many women choose isolation or no relationship at all.

When the Relationship Ends

Whether the daughter of a narcissistic mother is abandoned by her partner or leaves him herself, she feels great shame for the failed relationship. No matter if this is the first one or a series of failures, her sense of not being good enough deepens. Her self-esteem is greatly affected by relationship failures. In our society, a woman can fail at business or finances, but failures in relationships are less acceptable. Having more than one divorce or failed love relationship feels like a curse or a gross affliction. A woman will feel guilt and shame, but shame will be the emotion she finds most difficult. Guilt is usually associated with a deed that can be forgiven, but shame encompasses her being, taking on an "all or nothing" quality, which has devastating consequences for mental health. Adult daughters of narcissistic mothers often refer to themselves as "damaged" or "damaged goods," particularly after a series of failed love relationships. Underneath this shame is the feeling that they are unlovable.

- A beautiful client, Tyra, came to me after her second divorce. The epitome of beauty, intelligence, and charm, she reminds me of a petite china doll. But beneath her charming sweetness is a deep sense of sadness and unworthiness. She has recognized her past with a narcissistic mother, but now that her second husband has left her for another woman, she comes to therapy with this request: "Make me good enough!"

- Margo, 55, tells me, "I can hardly speak of this feeling of failure. I feel so damaged now. Who would ever want to even date me? How do you tell someone you have had more than two marriages? Do they not automatically think you are unhealthy or weird in some way? This is messed up and feels like it will never be better."

- Summer reports, "If I want to feel immense pain and shame, I think about my relationship history. This will do me in. I usually try not to even think about it or even let it come into my conscious being. Talk about feeling unlovable!"

- "No kidding, listen to this," says Karla when expressing her pain about relationships. "When I introduced my fiancé to my mother, she shook his hand and then said, 'Good luck. Hope you do better than the last one did.' How does one get over this shame of past failures in relationships?"

Why We Pick Who We Pick

Typically, the daughter of a narcissistic mother will choose a spouse who cannot meet her emotional needs. Even though our intuition will tell us in some way when something is not right for us, we tend to block it out if it isn't saying what we want to hear. When the hope for love blossoms, we override the intuitive inner voice or gut feeling.

Years of treating and interviewing daughters with maternal deprivation have shown me that we have a deep sense of intelligent intuition,
but it seems to be accompanied by a special brand of "deafness." In
the desperate search for love that did not exist in her childhood, the
daughter chooses not to pay attention to the red flags that may be
waving. We do know. We just don't listen. In recovery, you will learn
better how to tune in to your innate intuitive direction and guidance.

You actually "choose" a partner largely on an unconscious level.
As human beings we are attracted to the familiar. If you have not
worked out unfinished business with your mother, you will likely find
yourself with someone who re-creates that mother-daughter pattern
of behavior. We also tend to pick partners who are on the same emotional level we are.

If you are dependent, you feel this way with your partner: I am
going to lean on and be dependent on you. I see you as a person who
can do a lot for me. You can take care of me. You have money, pres-
tige, a good family and good job, you're gorgeous, you look good on
paper—you fit my list of criteria.

If you are codependent, you feel this way with your partner: I am
going to take care of you to the exclusion of taking care of myself. I
see you as someone I can feel needed by. You need me to nurture, take
care of you, and be a mother to you. You need my love because you
didn't get that as a child, you need my direction—you need me and
that makes me feel good.

Healthy relationships are based on an interdependency, where
both partners move back and forth in the caretaking, but mostly op-
erate as independent adults. This means that neither partner is dependent or codependent. In the dependent-codependent relationship,
neither partner loves the other for who he or she is as a person—they
act out roles and a distorted definition of love. An adult daughter of
a narcissistic mother is often misguided in her choices by her unre-
solved neediness. Need-based relationships are usually unfulfilling
because no one can satisfy all of an adult's unmet childhood needs.
But until the daughter addresses this empty void herself, she will ex-

pect that someone else can fill her with the feelings of worthiness, competence, and love that she lacks.

Many times the adult daughter will choose a partner who can't meet even reasonable emotional needs because she unconsciously wants someone who cannot be emotionally intimate or vulnerable. This is what is familiar to her and what she feels is safe and predictable. Until she enters recovery, she is not especially in touch with her own feelings and therefore needs to partner with someone who is not "into" the feelings realm either.

When a daughter's emotional and intimate needs are unmet, she can easily fall into the blame game, rather than own up to having chosen the wrong person. If this sounds familiar, be careful here: You do not want to fall into the narcissistic trap of viewing your partner as either good or bad. If you turn your idealized partner into a villain, you may then feel compelled to abandon him before he abandons you. Abandonment is a great fear because you felt abandoned. Your parents may have been there physically, but you felt emotionally abandoned. If you are dependent, it will be more difficult for you to leave the relationship. You might stay in an abusive or otherwise unwholesome partnership, feeling that you deserve no better. If you are abandoned by your partner, you might have an unusually difficult time recovering from the loss and rejection because it will trigger your past experience with Mother.

The Codependent Relationship

Overachievers often, unconsciously, find men who need to be taken care of. They are attracted to the "what I can do for you" dynamic. The daughter lets her well-learned skills of taking care of Mom and all her needs make her into a caretaker for life. When she partners with a man whom she can take care of in some way, she feels in a familiar, emotionally safe situation. A man who is dependent on her won't abandon her. In return for taking care of him, she hopes that he will in turn fill her void and emptiness. Of course, this never works, and what happens instead is: The more demanding, dependent, or immature the man is, the more he reminds her of her mother, who was extremely needy and had "entitlement" demands. She eventually feels resentment and anger and becomes overwhelmed. She runs around trying mightily to meet his needs in hopes of a return pass of the ball, but it never quite happens that way. She gets tired.

The adult daughter does not really trust the dependent partner or his capacity for intimacy, because she knows, at some level, that she chose him *because* he is not capable of vulnerability or emotional intimacy. She has thwarted her need for validation and her hope for authentic, loving connection. He cannot love her for who she *is*, and thus she is constantly frustrated and sad. She seeks love but cannot find it until she completes her recovery.

I use a basketball analogy in therapy to give a visual image of this couple. Imagine a basketball floor with a basket at each end and bleachers on the side of the floor. The codependent, usually high-achieving woman is running back and forth making all the baskets on both sides, while the partner is sitting in the bleachers watching and hoping she will win the game for them both. After a while, the woman gets exhausted, feels frustrated and resentful, and wants to stop. The partner in the bleachers might be content that someone else is doing all the work for him, but his self-esteem is getting no validation or elevation, as he is not doing his part for himself or his partner.

- Betsy made the most of the three-pointers in her marriage. "I have a high tolerance for deviant behavior. Codependency galore! I recognize it now. Looking back on my second husband, he was passive and nice, and I was willing to put up with anything because he was nice to me. I was more charismatic and more social, the breadwinner. He used me. He was narcissistic and had a narcissistic injury too. I kept busy and took care of everything. He got fired a lot because of verbal arguments with people. I always wrote his résumés and got his jobs for him. Looking back, I see that he didn't recognize what I did for him. He put no effort into things. He never said the words 'I'm sorry.' I had a high tolerance for this; I blew it off and went on with life. My expectation of others seems to be low. In relationships, I am comfortable with 80/20, not 50/50. I always give more than I get."

- Daria says, "The pattern I see with myself in love relationships is that the physical relationship is the most important. If I am not present in the most sexual way, I feel I will not receive love from my boyfriend. I am valued for what I do for him sexually. I got this from my mom. She was always so beautiful. She would get dressed for Dad. She smelled good, sexy lingerie, sex toys, tried to look good for Dad. Dad had *Playboy* magazines, and she would look through them with us. Sex was very important to their relationship. She taught me that what I can do for a man was how I would be valued by him."

- In every relationship, Coral has worked harder than the man. "I keep everything going when things don't work out. I feel responsible for everything. I don't hold him as accountable as I hold myself."

- "My pattern is to pick men I can control completely," Charlene says. "Then I can't get hurt. I pick people underneath me or less accomplished than I am. When I got married, I was screaming in my head, No, no, no. I knew then, but I kept going."

- Marlene says, "I always got into relationships with people who were messed up and needed me. My last boyfriend tried to kill himself when I broke up with him and had to be hospitalized. I always got the boys that were down on their luck. I do the same thing with girlfriends. I am everyone's adviser."

- Kate, 64, relates the following: "My relationship patterns are not good. I usually picked the wrong men. My first husband was abusive, physically and emotionally; my second husband was an alcoholic and a drug addict; and my third husband is an addict and felon. I smother, take care of them, and try to fix everything. I often get to a point where I have had enough and then I go on. I tend to try to impress and over-love somebody to make him love me."

- Margie is a single career woman. "My relationships are always kind of nonemotional. Kind of like a business, rather than an emotional connection. Not feeling fulfilled. Finding that there is something missing from that person that I could find elsewhere. Feeling the sensation of being trapped at times. I am the codependent, the caregiver. I've always wanted to be the dependent one."

- Dee Dee, 72, looks back at her marriage and her children. "I learned codependency. I see it with my husband and with my kids too. If I just do this or do that, you will love me more. I feel like I lost a lot of my identity and I am now finding myself again. My husband doesn't value me for who I am, only what I do for him. I've always been the pleaser, the peacemaker, making sure everything is okay and nobody is upset."

Until a woman has discovered and claimed her own sense of self, she will be frightened by a competent man who *can* actually meet her needs as she in turn meets his. A healthy man doesn't want to be controlled or mothered, and he also wants to give in return. He understands how to be interdependent. The codependent needs to understand

and realize that her behavior as a codependent is in truth her defense mechanism for her own dependency. It is her way to rail against these dependent needs and try to show that she is strong and in control and doesn't need anybody, when in reality, she does, as do we all.

It is much easier for the codependent to accept and face her issues than for the dependent, because the codependent looks stronger and more competent on the outside as she is running that basketball floor and making those baskets in victory. Who wants to admit that they are a dependent soul? Doesn't it sound better to say, "I am a caretaker," than to say, "I want someone to take care of me"? Dependents don't openly admit to this tendency and so they have a more difficult time getting in touch with this part of the narcissistic legacy. It is an eye-opener to most codependents, however, when they realize that their codependent behavior is a disguise for deeper unmet needs. They somehow have to see themselves as more powerful than they are to override the pain. In recovery, however, codependents do recognize their dependent issues.

The Dependent Relationship

The dependent daughter in a relationship is also looking for a partner to fill the emotional void and the emptiness left by a narcissistic mother. Her partner becomes the replacement for her mother, and he enacts the *what you can do for me* part of the relationship.

Relationships go through stages. The first stage can be characterized by feelings of "cloud nine" surreal fascination. I call this "la-la land," where the dependent daughter is in hog heaven. She has found a guy to take care of her and give her everything she didn't get in childhood—a dream come true! It looks perfect in the beginning because all conflict is put on the shelf and control given to her partner. What could be better? She didn't get the love she needed in childhood, and now Mr. Right is going to fulfill her every dream!

In the end, however, Mr. Right becomes Mr. Mistake. The dependent daughter has unconsciously chosen a man to take care of her who will likely become codependent. She will end up stifling him with her overwhelming demands, jealousy, and insecurities. She will want him to be with her at all times and expect him to meet all her needs, particularly her emotional needs. When he cannot do this, she will be angry, like her mother had been, which will confuse and frustrate her partner. The daughter, too, will end up in a lot of pain as she reenacts her relationship with her narcissistic mother in a role reversal. She will feel the same disappointment and emptiness she felt as a child, and blame her spouse for not being good enough for her. Her sense of entitlement will spring into action, resembling Mom as she rails, "If you love me, you will do these things for me, and I deserve and expect this [entitlement]."

- Lise recalls that she stayed uninvolved in her early years and had lots of partners. "I never let anyone get too close. When I did get married at age 31, it was all about what he could do for me. When he couldn't do for me, I left. It had to be my way or the highway."

- Sarah Jo, 44, relates, "My emptiness shows up in my relationships. My empty feeling seems to go away when someone is enamored with me and I get a honeymoon feeling; then, when it is not there, I feel empty. It takes on a somatic element—I physically feel heaviness in my chest. Not cardiac, have had it tested. It physically feels like a hole."

- Dawn, 30, says, "I choose men who can't love me—the emotionally unavailable types. My mother did this too. I do it on a grander scale, quantity wise, and my grandmother did the same thing. Then I have to work really hard at not being too needy as my dependency kicks in."

Although we have seen the distinct patterns of the codependent and the dependent adult daughter, it is important to understand that you can switch back and forth between these two relationship dynamics depending on where you are emotionally at the time. You can do this within one relationship; you can also become one or the other with different men. Although this sounds confusing, it is best understood this way: The daughter of a narcissistic mother has unmet needs and therefore displays some neediness. The codependent behavior is a disguise to cover up the neediness and display strength and competence. When under stress, her neediness will come out and she will look like the dependent.

The Loner

The loner wears different hats, some healthy, some not. As a part of recovery it is often advised that the daughter of a narcissistic mother spend some time alone to focus on herself and learn how to fulfill her needs for herself. She may need to slow down for a while to accomplish this healthy "loner time." Even if she is married or in a relationship, she can spend some time alone in order to work on her authentic self.

The unhealthy loner, however, is the daughter who has decided she is so damaged or unlovable that she can never be in a relationship. Usually because she has had a series of bad relationships, she has given up on herself. She wants to have love in her life, but believes nothing can change and decides to just go it alone from here on out. She has great fears of connecting again because she is aware that her "relationship picker" has been damaged by her narcissistic mother's messages, and this fear prevents her from finding what she wants in a love relationship. She avoids the dating scene, is lonely but stays alone anyway, and her feeling of "I'm not good enough" becomes a mantra for her life.

- Marcia, 59, trusts no one but her dog. "I am angry that I have spent the best years of my adult life in unhealthy relationships trying to capture the love and approval my mother withheld. Only because my life exploded on all fronts did I gain the perspective that I had been blind to the recurrences of unhealthy childhood dynamics. I'm nearly 60 years old now, so much life has gone by, and I'm basically alone today. Guess what? I'm staying that way! It's far too risky to do anything else."

Having been there myself for a time, I know that this woman just needs to complete her own recovery. When she does, the world will look better. I tell my clients that you cannot trust men without trusting yourself and your "relationship picker." You can't have the word TR_ST without the letter U. Hanging in there and reviving yourself is the answer for this kind of loner. I'll show you some ways to restore your faith in your own intuition.

Another kind of loner has made a conscious decision after recovery to spend her life without a love relationship. She truly has no fears barring the way to a relationship and her decision is a healthy one. I don't know many women who do this, but the ones I do know are in a state of self-fulfillment; they have made a good decision for themselves. Who can argue with this? Even if most do not choose this route, it can be a healthy place to be.

Post-Romantic Stress

> She did not know how to love me and I don't know how to love you.
>
> —Sidda Walker, in
> *Divine Secrets of the Ya-Ya Sisterhood*[2]

• Savannah, 38, relates, "When I met my husband, I wouldn't let him in emotionally. It took me years to feel the love for him that I have now. I didn't love him then the way I am able to now. Or my children. It took time to learn it. I used to feel it for my cat, but not for people. All my feelings were numb, even the good ones."

In summary, daughters of narcissistic mothers face a number of serious struggles in love relationships, including shame and feelings of not being good enough. Relationship failures are often the main reason they seek therapy in the first place: They don't understand why they keep making the same mistakes and they fear that their "stupidity" in choosing the wrong men can never be rectified. You may know how painful this can be for yourself, your sister, or your friends. Many of my clients are in a state of hopelessness and depression when they begin therapy, but I am always happy to inform them that there is good news and hope. When a daughter chooses to invest in herself, face the wounded childhood and history, and complete the recovery process (to come in part 3), things begin to change. Learning to stop the repetition compulsion, to separate from your mother, build your own sense of self, and free yourself from the damaging internalized messages, you set out on a whole new healthy, optimistic journey. My client Kimberly puts it like this:

- "I have worked through the deep-rooted narcissistic abuse from my childhood, so I am now living a happier life with myself, my son, my husband and family. I have given up the old hope of getting my mother's love. In turn, the love in my heart is overflowing and more powerful than I ever imagined possible."

We are almost ready for the recovery section to see how Kimberly and others have accomplished the above. But before we do that, there's one more arena we must take a look at: what happens when we become mothers ourselves.

CHAPTER NINE

HELP!
I'M BECOMING MY MOTHER
DAUGHTERS AS MOTHERS

I keep praying that I am saving for my children's college
education and not for their therapy.
—Bonnie, 38

G iving birth to a child is a life-altering experience. When your
first child enters the world, you enter the new state of "perma-
nent parenthood" and remain there forever. For most women, the
experience of bearing a child is blessed with intoxicating excitement and anticipatory visions for the future. For daughters of narcissistic mothers, however, it can also be blighted by unrelenting fear
and anxiety.

The fear is of being like Mother, of emotionally orphaning your
children or harming them in some other way. You worry about not
feeling good enough to do the job—whether because you carry that
nagging belief around with you everywhere, or because you know
you lack certain skills you will need as a parent. Perhaps you haven't
yet fully come into your own identity. Whatever its origin, your fear
is very real.

- Mattie's apprehensions about becoming a mother brought her into therapy. "Getting pregnant was the scariest thing ever for me. I didn't have a need to be pregnant and have kids. I wasn't even sure I wanted kids. I was worried that I would be a horrible mother, like mine was, emotionally and physically abusive. Would I be? What if I turned out to be just as crazy as she?"

- For Kylie, having a child brought back many memories of her childhood. "My mother did not connect with me. I felt like she never saw me." Kylie felt that she had to give her daughter what she hadn't received. "Whenever my daughter would make a sound," she told me, "I would say, 'I see you, Lacy. I see you.' "

- Lavonda reports, "I was so excited when I first got pregnant but very worried, too, that I was going to mess up my kids. I did a lot of therapy while I was pregnant and wanted to have a big talk with my mom then, but my therapist advised me not to. I so wanted my mother to hear me, but my therapist made me realize it was unlikely that this would happen. I mostly worried that I would be narcissistic too. I don't want to smother my baby like my mother did me."

- As a young adult, Mia felt very much alone. "I was alone, sad, empty, and involved with drugs and alcohol. I would picture having a family and cry about it. Since I've had my own family, I don't feel quite so empty, but I know I fill the emptiness by being the mother that I *wanted* rather than the mother that I *had*."

- Sidney relates this story: "I still have fears that I will be like her. My ex-husband says that I have traits of my mother. One time, he said I looked like her because I was smoking a little cigarillo, and he said, 'You are just as pretentious as your mother.' I never touched those again. I turned pale and put it out. I just hope I am not like my mother in my parenting style!"

To have worries and fears about your parenting is normal, but the women above have concerns that are a few steps beyond those of most mothers-to-be. Of course, we strive to do the right things for our children, and none of us wants to pass along our own undesirable legacy. Breaking the cycle is a challenge when you have no positive role model as a mother. Daughters of narcissistic mothers often feel as if we are blazing our own trail of love in raising *our* babies.

If you see yourself making mistakes in parenting, don't panic. You don't have to be afraid even if you have learned or inherited some narcissistic parenting traits. This does not mean that you are narcissistic. You *can* change. The best thing you can do for yourself and your family is to allow yourself the awareness of possible mistakes you could make or have made, and work to correct them. This chapter is designed specifically to look at the pitfalls many of us face.

Warning: The Risk of Doing the Opposite

If a daughter swings to the other end of the continuum and acts the opposite of her mother, she stands a good chance of creating the same dynamics that she's trying so hard to avoid. The key lies in finding a middle ground on which you can stand as a loving parent with your own values.

Typically when we want to change something, we think in black and white terms. Let's say you want to work on explosive anger and aggressive behavior. You switch to the opposite end of the emotional spectrum and start behaving in passive, meek, quiet, nonassertive ways. Being explosively angry means you are stuffing feelings until they explode, and being passive and nonassertive probably means you are not expressing your emotions either. Your goal is to go to the middle and become assertive, but it takes a while to get there.

If you want to parent in different ways from your mother, remember that the middle ground you find ultimately needs to be based on *your* value system and beliefs, but it can indeed include some of your mother's beliefs. For instance: Maybe you like a clean house, as did your mother, or you plan to stay with the same religious denomination, or have strong beliefs about the importance of education, but you want to parent with a special ear for your child's emotional needs, which is likely very different from your mother. You don't completely throw the baby out with the bathwater and just go the total opposite direction with everything. We begin to see mistakes when we do this.

If you had an engulfing mother, for instance, you may decide you will absolutely not be a smothering mother, but end up doing the opposite, so the child feels ignored on some level. Jaime tried too hard not to smother her daughter, Chelsea, and on the first day of kindergarten her little girl, who had just turned five, was found crying in the classroom. She wanted her mother to sit with the class for a while like some of the other parents. Jaime, bound and determined not to be an overprotective mom like her own mother, had gone overboard the opposite way.

If you had an ignoring mother, you may decide to give your child so much attention that you end up engulfing her. Rosaline found that she could not let her child alone. "I had to be involved in everything she did and everywhere she went because I was so afraid she would think I didn't care like I felt with my mother. When she was twelve, she set me straight by telling me to get a life, as she was kind of sick of me."

Another example may be how you handle praising your child. You were never praised or encouraged, so you overdo it with your children. Terra created a situation where her daughter not only felt entitled, but also believed she could never measure up. "My sixteen-year-old broke down in tears the other day. I sat with her immediately and began to tell her all the wonderful things I could think of and how awesome she was. I found out that I was 'overpraising' her and she felt like she was a fake in trying to please me and that she could never measure up to all the things I thought about her. Damn. I over-did it, I guess. I was trying to be so different from my mother."

- Marlene's mother was very strict and did not allow her children the freedom of speech, space, and choices they needed. She decided to be super lenient with her children, and they turned out to be kids with no boundaries, unable to manage their own behavior. "I was bound and determined to let my kids be. I wanted them to feel total freedom and not be caged and stifled like I was as a child. But I soon discovered that all that freedom led two of my daughters to getting in trouble with the law and enough speeding tickets and accidents to break my pocketbook in insurance and car repair bills. I guess I should not have gone that far."

This is tricky business. Parenting is tough, and of course none of us do it perfectly, but these stories show how easy it is to pass along a dysfunction when we think we are doing exactly the opposite of how we were reared.

Modeling the Not-Good-Enough Message

Sometimes we are able to find that middle ground and what we do with our children reflects that. If you succeeded in this, give yourself credit; you deserve lots of it. One pitfall to finding the middle ground, however, is the internal belief that we ourselves are *not good enough*. If you carry this unhealthy message within yourself, you are most likely modeling it for your children. You will show them inadver-tently, through your behavior, that you feel unworthy, and they will grow to feel the same way about themselves. This can happen even if you don't really believe it or ever say it to them. Remember, children learn more through what they see in us than through what we tell them. If you model in yourself a woman who does not take good care of herself or who stays in unhealthy relationships, feeling you don't deserve better, or you do not pursue your own passions, don't be surprised if you see the same in your children. Similarly, if you set boundaries and stand up for yourself, your children most likely will too. This is the best reason there is to embrace recovery.

How Do You Spell "Empathy"?

Many daughters who didn't get empathy from their mothers do not know how to give it to their children. The ability to empathize is the most important parenting skill there is. Nothing makes you feel more real, heard, and understood than someone who empathizes with you in a time of need.

If this skill was neither modeled nor taught well in your family of origin, you will need to work to develop it. Shay, a pensive, insightful, and highly educated woman who was raised by an ignoring narcissistic mother, has four children now and a loving husband. They were all in my office for family therapy to learn about healthy communication following a suicide in their extended family that had frightened them all. Every single family member present that day was committed, but Shay was particularly worried. Aware of her unmet childhood needs with her own mother, she didn't have a clue how to empathize with her own children, who told her, in session, that she "sucked" at this. Shay spent many months working on developing the skill of expressing empathy.

Kami, 45, came to therapy to increase her empathy for her seventeen-year-old daughter, who was pregnant. She realized she was having trouble being there for her child. An insightful, intelligent woman raised by an image-oriented narcissistic mother, Kami found herself overly concerned about what her friends and family would think. She was not narcissistic, was aware of her childhood issues, but still couldn't shake some of her ingrained messages. She seemed to talk to me from two sides of her being. One side was angry, humiliated, and shamed by her daughter's actions, and the other side was humane and loving and wanted to do right by her. She clearly did the right thing in seeking assistance in how to let her own issues rest and tune in to her daughter's needs at the time. Today Kami is a proud grandmother, and her daughter speaks highly of her mother's nurturing ability.

My Kid the Honor Student

How many of these bumper stickers have we seen? Where are the bumper stickers that say "My kid has a big heart," "My kid is honest," "My kid is kind"? A significant problem I see in my practice today is too many parents unable or unwilling to tune in to who their child is as a person. As a daughter of a narcissistic mother, you should beware of this major pitfall. Your child's accomplishments are not who your child is.

Abbie, 47, came to a therapy session worried about her son who was the quarterback on the high school football team, first chair in an honors band, an honor student, and a great-looking kid to boot. Eventually she reported that this great kid had just been arrested and was in juvenile detention for pointing a gun at another student at a lakeside party over the weekend. When she went to visit him in jail, he was crying and told her that he felt too much pressure to succeed in everything and always felt he had to be the best. He wanted to prove that he was just a normal guy who got in trouble sometimes. While this kind of getting in trouble was over the edge, Abbie learned to see past the accomplishments and into her son's anxieties and fears.

Dori was worried about her daughter because the fourteen-year-old had just been picked up for shoplifting: "How can this kid, who is a total star in her musical abilities, be doing such a stupid thing as shoplifting? She has a recital on Friday. How could she?"

Obviously Dori should have been thinking more along the lines of "What is going on in my young daughter's feelings? What does she feel she is missing? Does she not feel worthy? There has to be a reason that she is sabotaging her talent and I want to find out why." At the time, Dori had a way to go in learning empathy.

Those Messy Things Called Feelings

It's easy to understand the need for authenticity until your own child shows authentic feelings and you don't like what she is saying or feeling. This is particularly difficult if she expresses negative feelings about you. Allowing authenticity in children will be discussed more in part 3, but here are some examples of how not allowing your child to be authentic can get you in trouble as a parent.

Alexis, who had been taught as a child not to deal with authentic feelings, has two daughters, both of whom are now involved in drugs. She came to therapy asking for help without having ever talked to her daughters about this issue. I asked her if she had confronted the drug abuse, and she told me, "Oh, no, what would I say to them? Do I really want to know?"

Fiona's thirteen-year-old daughter recently informed her that she had been sexually abused. The girl had been afraid to tell her mother the real story because the perpetrator was a family member. Fiona came to therapy wanting not to believe her daughter and to shove the whole issue under the rug. I worked with Fiona so that she could listen to her little girl and get to the bottom of what had happened to her. Lack of authenticity can truly be dangerous.

My Daughter, My Friend

You may be thinking, "I want to have my daughter as a friend. I crave this closeness. I didn't have this with my mother. Please don't tell me this is wrong. What is the right way?" Even when your daughter becomes an adult, you must still be the mother. You will continue to have parenting duties and need to provide guidance, empathy, and understanding. It is not your daughter's job to give that to you.

Jan, a mother of three girls, brought her oldest two to therapy because they were displaying signs of anger that she didn't understand. I asked Jan to leave the room so I could sit with the girls and chat. As soon as Jan left my office, the girls both made a disgusting gesture toward her. I knew then we were in for some kind of mother-daughter train wreck. I had expected that the girls were probably not getting the cell phones, cars, clothes or freedom they wanted, but the issue was very different. They both told me that Jan expected them to help her get over her depression, and they were totally exasperated and feeling helpless. They reported that each day when they came home from school, they sat with their mother and listened to her sadness, crying, and desperation and they were sick of it. Jan had grown up with a psychosomatic narcissistic mother, so she knew better, but she was falling into a similar pattern with her children in expecting them to take care of her emotionally. Luckily, the situation was easily turned around and Jan went back into psychotherapy. However, one can see that, even with education and awareness, adult daughters of narcissistic mothers can unwittingly fall into the legacy of narcissistic behaviors.

Take Care of Yourself but Stay Connected to Others

Although healthy self-care is central to the recovery of daughters of narcissistic mothers, self-care does not mean becoming self-absorbed. Taking care of yourself does not mean tuning out others' feelings. I have seen daughters make the mistake of misinterpreting self-care to mean they should focus on themselves in unhealthy ways, even after they saw how harmful their mother's belief was that everything was "all about Mom."

Marni had three children at home, but decided that instead of giving those children the time and attention they needed, her recovery mission was to take care of herself with luxurious clothing, fancy trips, and expensive jewelry. When her kids were brought to therapy for acting out and getting in trouble with the law, she was on the beach somewhere getting a nice suntan. The kids were angry and also surprised because this was not typical behavior. Again, Marni knew better and had done some of her own recovery work but had not understood this part very well. Family therapy was very effective, because as soon as she heard how her children were feeling, she set about to truly understand what she needed to do for herself and them.

Healthy self-care means finding fulfillment so that you have energy, love, and empathy for others. Finding the middle ground means realizing that it is not an either-or situation—you are neither full of self nor drained of self.

Part 3 will teach you how to do this. Having established an understanding of how maternal narcissism creates certain negative dynamics in the mother-daughter relationship that affect daughters' lives as adults, we are now ready to step onto the path to recovery.

ENDING THE LEGACY

Specific Recovery Steps
for Daughters of Narcissistic Mothers

Now that you have an understanding of how the behavior of your mother affected you, you can begin to heal by taking the following steps to recover from the pain:

- Accept your mother's limitations and grieve that you did not have the mother you wanted
- Separate psychologically from your mother, and reframe the negative messages that you absorbed from her into positive ones
- Develop and accept your own identity, feelings, and desires
- Deal with your mother in a different, healthy manner
- Work to recognize your own narcissistic traits and refuse to pass them on to your children.

The next chapters will guide you through the steps of recovering from a narcissistic mother. In part 1, you began to understand and identify the problems that a child learns to deal with when she has a narcissistic mother. Part 2 helped you see how these problems follow you into adulthood. Now, in part 3, you will see how to accept your past, allow yourself to feel grief about it, reprogram negative messages that you've internalized, reframe your beliefs and views, and change your life.

CHAPTER TEN

First Steps

HOW IT FEELS, NOT HOW IT LOOKS

I wish there were a mental health diagnosis for serial grief.
I am not mentally ill. Mostly just sad and grieving the
vision of the mother I so desperately wanted.
—Sonny, 39

As a child growing up, you were likely very good at denying, numbing, or compensating for your own feelings rather than allowing yourself to feel them. You probably do this now as an adult too. Your recovery begins in this chapter. Here I will guide you to reclaim your emotions and enhance your sense of self.

Now that you have a solid understanding of the psychological dynamics you were subject to as a daughter of a narcissistic mother and how they have adversely affected your life, it is time for you to come to terms with the past, release your unrealistic expectations of your mother, and take charge of your life to heal. Now it's your time to make your life more peaceful and comfortable.

You will follow the blueprint for healing in this chapter that I used for my own recovery and continue to use for my clients. It works if you follow the steps sequentially. You will feel worlds better than you ever have. However, it is important to note that you cannot completely "cure" the scars of a childhood trauma. You work with them, process them, and learn how to deal with them differently so that you feel better.

I liken our lives to a tree. Each of us, like a tree, has roots (our upbringing); long, sturdy trunks (our development); and branches that flower and grow in our adult lives. Your trunk or development phase bears the scars, which don't really go away; they are part of who we are. But recovery work helps us to treat any gashes, to fill them in, supply balm and seal them gently, and takes away the old and recurring pain, changing the original trauma, allowing you to grow around it and up and away from it. Please keep this in mind, so that you do not become discouraged and misled. Really, it is a relief to know that you don't have to totally remove those scars. The things

Our Growth and Development

Adults
Branching
Budding
Flowering
Growing
Changing

Trauma Scars

Our Roots
Family of Origin and Generational Legacy

that happened to us are important to acknowledge; they play into who we are today. Yet they do not define who we are today, and by working in recovery, you refuse to allow your past to tell you who you are. You accept and face your past as part of you, and you move on.

I believe that you begin to heal when you accept the fact that your mother was narcissistic and that she hurt you. Then you grieve for the life and love you do not have. I will teach you how to allow yourself the gift of acceptance and how to use the precious time for grieving. Read on for assistance in how to do this.

Three-Step Recovery Model

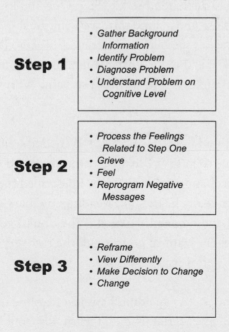

Step 1
- *Gather Background Information*
- *Identify Problem*
- *Diagnose Problem*
- *Understand Problem on Cognitive Level*

Step 2
- *Process the Feelings Related to Step One*
- *Grieve*
- *Feel*
- *Reprogram Negative Messages*

Step 3
- *Reframe*
- *View Differently*
- *Make Decision to Change*
- *Change*

The Three Steps of Recovery

Recovery entails three steps. The first step is to understand the problem, to diagnose it, and to get the background information that defines it. This is true for any emotional or psychological issue you may deal with in your life. This is what a therapist works on with you in the beginning of a therapeutic relationship. You've just completed Step One—you've read about the problem and how it plays out in symptoms and life patterns. This is the cognitive or intellectual understanding that you will need to go on to the next steps.

In Step Two, you process the feelings related to the identified problem. That is what this chapter is about. As a daughter of a narcissistic mother you had feelings that were not often validated or acknowledged. The earlier sections of the book helped you to identify them, and now it is time to work with those feelings.

I am going to tell you something very important that I have learned in 28 years of being a therapist: Most people like to skip Step Two—this step. Daughters tend to like Step One and love Step Three of recovery. But, most understandably, we want to skip the most important step that makes the biggest difference, because it is painful to wade through the marshes of past trauma. It is difficult to push through the denial and let yourself feel the pain. Who wants to feel pain, right?

- Lauren, 31, said to me in therapy, "Why does reliving all of this make me so angry? I really got the short end of the stick. Why did this happen to me? When I described the ideal mom to you, it made my heart sink. Reading my diary to you, it hurt so bad and made me so mad. Why don't I get an apology? I don't want to go through the recovery process. I just want to get over it!"

- Elyse, 54, states, "As an adult, I am just learning to be in touch with my feelings. I certainly didn't learn this from Mom. I can still picture her and how controlled she was with feelings. She would put on her sunglasses and get this stone-cold face. If I got emotional, she would say, 'Stop it or I'll slap you!' "

Nonetheless, the second step is where you get to learn how to deal with those difficult things called feelings. It's not fun, but it's worth it.

When Lauren, Elyse, other clients, and I allowed this grief process, we began to see how we could finally let go.

Processing feelings is very different from just talking about them. To process means to talk about the trauma, and simultaneously feel the pain in a cacophonous, blasting, rock concert. You can tell something in a story form without feeling it, but that is not processing. This is the only way to release trauma from your body. For example, I can tell you about going to my grandmother's funeral and fill you in on details about her death, the service, the people, the family, the minister, the flowers, and the travel, etc., but this is *talking* about the funeral and her death. It is describing the events. If I were processing it, I would be telling you the same story but feeling the loss and the grief at the same time. In this very different scenario, you would see my tears and feel my pain, and so would I, as I described the situation and how it affected me. This chapter will help you, too, engage in this kind of grieving.

When people skip Step Two of recovery, Step Three does not work. I believe that this is why many therapeutic programs are unsuccessful, because folks skip the middle, the difficult part. We have to clean out trauma before we can learn to look at our situation in a healthy and different way.

Step Three, briefly, is about "reframing," a therapeutic word that means looking at the problem through another set of lenses, or in a new way. This is the fun part of recovery, when you begin to see things differently and become free of the symptoms and the effects of the trauma of having had a narcissistic mother. You make decisions for yourself that are very different from when you were feeling like a victim of wrongdoing. You begin to get in touch with your real feelings, values, and belief system. You find the authentic you and allow it to function in your own way. This is freedom, and I wish this for each reader who is with me here.

A Closer Look at Recovery

We move now to specifics for healing the unmothered child. The five basic areas to be covered in part 3 of this book are listed here for easy reference:

1. Accepting your mother's limitations, and allowing yourself to grieve
2. Separating psychologically from Mother, and reframing the negative messages
3. Working on your authentic sense of self
4. Dealing with Mother and your relationship with her in a healthy way
5. Treating your own narcissistic traits and refusing to pass on the legacy to your own children.

Let's begin with acceptance.

Acceptance of Mother's Limitations

To realize that your own mother may not be capable of real love and empathy is shocking. If you ever allowed yourself to think this before, you might have been unwilling to accept it. Mothers are supposed to be the most reliable source of love, comfort, and empathy, and if your mother did not provide that for you, you most likely denied your feelings about it. Daughters often blame themselves for their mother's inability to love them. Remember my client who said, "If my own mother can't love me, who can?" Accepting their mother's limitations is difficult for all daughters.

- Martina, 25, says, "My mind has given up on having a loving relationship with Mom. I have 25 years of evidence, but in my *heart* it hasn't sunk in for real. It's a twofold thing. When she is nice to me, shopping for suits for work, or chairs for the house or paint chips, I get lulled back into it. I get my hopes up that maybe this time will be different."

- Many daughters never give up the hope. Sandy, 32, claims, "I always wanted a normal mom. One who doesn't dress like a hooker, who doesn't flirt with your boyfriends, who has normal holidays, who loves me and my boyfriend and showers us both in love, goes on family trips and has fun; one who doesn't compete with me and isn't threatened by me and is proud of my achievements and what I have done. Do I have to give up on all of this?"

Before you can grieve, you have to accept the reality of what you have gone through. Think of it like this: A teacher trying to teach a three-year-old to read at college level might feel disappointment, anger, even shame at his failure to accomplish this goal, until he realizes, of course, that the student is not really capable of the task. Most narcissists lack the capacity to give significant, authentic love and empathy, and you have no choice but to deal with this reality. Accepting that your own mother has this limited capacity is the first step. Let go of the expectation that it will ever be different.

Most daughters I know have gone through long periods in their lives not understanding this, always wishing and hoping that the next encounter with their mother will be different. This sets up not only unrealistic expectations for the daughter, but encourages her to keep going back to try again, for which the reward is additional sadness, disappointment, pain, anger, and exasperation. After all, we are talking about your mother—the person who was the center of your world and whom you loved and needed more than anyone else. I want to acknowledge again how difficult this is to do, but you must do it so you can move on toward your own recovery.

Remember also that narcissism is a spectrum disorder and our mothers may have varying degrees of narcissism. Mothers with fewer narcissistic traits are more likely to have some hope of recovery if they are motivated to do so. But the further along the spectrum your mother is, the more likely it is that she will not change or seek treatment and therefore you must accept this fact.

Many of my clients wonder, "How do I do that?" Remember that you cannot change others. You can change only yourself. How you view things and how you deal with your perceptions is within your control. Changing your mother is not. You may wish that you could drag your mother to therapy with you, and many women do that. Sometimes this is worth pursuing, sometimes not.

In all events, however, the success of the recovery work rests entirely with you, the daughter. Let go of the belief that your mother can or will be different, and will ever be able to give you the love you deserve. Letting go will free you and allow you to find yourself. Decide to accept and realize that Mom's inability, her incapacity, her illness, her limitations have hurt you. This beginning step takes you out of denial and forces you to deal with reality. It is a move toward health. Decide now. This act will give you back the control you need to pursue the important grief process that follows.

How Do I Know I Have Totally Accepted Mother's Limitations?

To determine where you are in this process of accepting your mother's limitations, you can ask yourself the following questions:

1. Do I continue to wish and hope that my mother will be different each time I talk to her?
2. Do I continue to have expectations of my mother?
3. Have I accepted my mother for who she is?
4. Am I expecting someone else to meet my childlike needs because I have given up on my mother?
5. Do I continue to try to get my childlike needs met in relationships instead of relying on myself?

6. Am I looking for a man to replace my mother?
7. Do I feel a sense of entitlement about my needs?
8. Am I now relying on myself to meet most of my needs, and when someone else is there for me, do I see it as an added blessing rather than my due?

When you have successfully completed the acceptance part of recovery, you realize that no one can really meet your childhood needs, and you choose number eight above. The part of life when you were entitled to that kind of maternal nurturing is gone. You are willing to grieve the loss but fully understand that you can't go back and get it and you can't make it happen now with someone else. Remember, as an adult, you are not entitled to this. You are responsible for yourself, now willing to accept this accountability for your own needs and to find a way to meet them. With this in place, you are ready to grieve.

Teach Yourself to Grieve

Deal with your feelings before they deal with you.
—The rehab counselor in the movie
Postcards from the Edge[1]

The grief process begins with another decision: to let your feelings be there. I had to teach myself how to do this, particularly when my feelings were sad or angry. As I learned to feel, there were some days when I would stay home from work, send the children to school, close the blinds, get the pillows, and just let myself cry, scream, hit pillows, or do whatever I needed to do to let out steam. At first, I just sat there and no feelings would surface, but I knew that there were mounds of feelings because they would come out in other ways when I least expected them. Eventually, giving myself this time, my tears would begin to leak and then pour. The trick was to let them be. To feel them.

This is difficult when you have been taught to stuff it or suck it up or not to feel anything, to be phony, to pretend everything is all right when it isn't.

Sit with those feelings. Sit with the pain. Manage the anxiety and depression that come with it so you can work through it. Don't try to talk yourself out of it. Others around you may try to do this. No one wants to see you hurt, and your loved ones may not understand how important this is, so don't listen to them. Let yourself feel! When the old denial tries to reassert itself, or the critical internal messages begin again, chase them away. Tell yourself that you deserve this time to heal.

It is common for you to feel like a wimp or to call yourself a baby. I do this on a regular basis, even now when I have feelings to process. I have to tell myself, "It's okay to be a baby right now. Babies are sweet and innocent." You won't be a baby forever, I promise. It doesn't last, because you work through it in this very way.

You may begin to try to rationalize away the pain. "I shouldn't feel this way," or "I didn't have it that bad." This won't help. Whatever is there you need to release. Let it be. Sometimes in order to do this you have to be quiet and take time to be alone. If you are used to keeping busy to avoid the pain, or to using a substance or some addiction to numb the pain, you will notice the feelings coming up when you slow down and sit quietly or allow yourself to be alone. This is very important to do. Set aside some time alone solely for this grieving process. Do it several times until you begin to feel relief.

Try several different things until you find what works for you. I do best when I am home alone with shades drawn. Some women like to take long walks, go for long runs, hike in the mountains, go for long drives, or sit in coffee shops. Everyone is different, and it is important for you to find your comfort zone. The most important thing is that you allow it to happen. Having been taught *not* to do this, daughters of narcissistic mothers at first feel awkward giving themselves this emotional attention. But you can do it.

The Stages of Grief

The natural grief process as written about by Dr. Elisabeth Kübler-Ross in *On Death and Dying* consists of five stages: denial, anger, bargaining, depression, and acceptance.[2] For your recovery, we will be using these stages, too, but we put acceptance first. We have already been engaged in denial and bargaining with Mother for a long time, and without acceptance we cannot move on to deal with our true feelings. Without acceptance, we stay in denial. After acceptance, we can process the anger and depression of our loss so that we can free ourselves from the pain we have felt over a lifetime. Let's look at some examples of how this works for us.

OUR STAGES OF GRIEF

1. *Acceptance.* We have to accept first that Mother has limited love and empathy to give, or we cannot allow ourselves out of the denial and learn how to feel our feelings. Acceptance is our first step in recovery, after we have realized our problem.
2. *Denial.* As children, we had to deny that our mothers were incapable of love and empathy so we could survive. A child yearns for love above all else, and we needed the denial to keep growing and surviving.
3. *Bargaining.* We have been bargaining our whole life with Mother, both internally and with her. We have been wishing and hoping that she will change, that she will be different the next time we need her. We have tried many things over the years to win her love and approval.
4. *Anger.* We feel intense anger and sometimes rage when we realize that our emotional needs were not met and that this neglect has affected our lives in severe, adverse ways. We feel angry at Mother and ourselves for allowing patterns to develop and for being stuck.
5. *Depression.* We feel intense sadness that we have to let go of the hope for and the vision of the kind of mother we wanted.

We realize that she will never be as loving as we want her to be. We feel like orphans or unmothered children. We let go of all expectations. We grieve the loss of the vision of these expectations.

During this grief process, you will bounce around through all the stages, back and forth. Don't move on until you solidly accept that your mother was indeed narcissistic and did not give you the love you needed and wanted. For only then can you properly grieve. If you find yourself not accepting, go back and work on it again. It is the prerequisite for the work to come.

Use a Journal

Using a journal to get through the recovery process will help you immensely. Throughout this recovery program, I will be referring to how writing things down in a journal keeps everything in one place. Journaling is a way to record the feelings that are coming to the surface and also helps you to review them and check on your progress. Some daughters like to write things out longhand, while others are more comfortable typing a computer journal. I have a grief file on my computer that I visit at the end of each day. There I can dump feelings that have surfaced that I need to deal with. Writing down feelings is another way of getting them out of your system, and by journaling you are reinforcing the release of your trauma. Do not worry about spelling, grammar, or sentence structure. Just write whatever is coming up for you.

Many daughters have resisted using a journal at first because they do not like to write or they are fearful of someone finding the information. Nonetheless, I encourage you to use a journal because it means you are taking your recovery seriously. You commit to writing down, keeping track of it, and monitoring your progress. Your health and happiness are worth this investment of time. You want to take control of your own healing and deal consciously with these lifelong feelings or they will control you.

Grieving the Mother You Never Had

Every little girl deserves to have a mother who is crazy about her. If you didn't have a loving mother, you have a right to grieve the loss.

As you let feelings come up, recognize them, and write them down. Start with a list of what the ideal mother would look like to you. Think about either what you wanted or what you saw in other mothers you know. Contrast what you wanted to what you had with your own mother. Face the disappointments and the pain you felt. This is extremely important at this phase of the recovery. Find the holes. Write them down. It is okay to do this.

Some women wrote the following in their ideal mom list:

- "I would want to have someone I could call and tell things to. Someone who understood me. I could talk to her about my feelings and she wouldn't say a thing about herself."

- "I would want a mom to talk about me and be proud of me in real ways, in accepting ways. Interested in things that I am interested in. Caring about my stuff. Acknowledging me. Not everything has to be about her."

- "I always wanted to be able to let down and tell her the truth and know that she would take care of me. I wanted to have feelings and have her stand there and feel them too. Tell her stuff and have her handle it and not make things worse. The ability to comfort me, protect me."

- "I wanted a mom who had a clue about my life, not one who was distant and unsupportive. I wanted her to ask about and care about her grandchildren. Every year or two she asks me how I am. Would sure want that different."

- "I so wanted and needed a mom who dealt with real feelings and was strong emotionally. A mom who let me develop my real self and didn't expect me to be such a showpiece for her. Some empathy and comforting would have been a blessing, and I can't even imagine that with her."

Even though most daughters feel sad that they did not receive the proper love from their mothers, they have a deep belief system ingrained from childhood that they do not or did not deserve a loving mother. But you deserve it! And if you didn't have this love, you must acknowledge that you didn't get it and that, as a result, you have this hole, a void, in your emotional development. Facing this sadness is crucial to developing your sense of self today. I'm not saying that you become permanently sad about this, but that you recognize it, face it, and allow yourself to feel sad about the pain this has caused you. We will move beyond this stage of grief. This is not where you will live the rest of your life.

Don't listen to others as you go through this process. Well-meaning friends and loved ones often say things like "Forget it already." "You can't undo the past—quit trying." "Quit thinking about the past and be in the present." Those closest to you (and some not so close) will discourage you from doing this important work because they do not understand just how important it is. They may not want to see you suffer, so they try to fix it. They don't understand that if you don't face this sadness, it will remain part of you forever. Do not listen to this unqualified advice. This is precisely why so many people today are projecting their feelings, misbehaving, creating crises for themselves and others, suffering from depression and anxiety, and are not being accountable for their own actions and emotions—they're not facing the truth about their own pain. I am giving you, from personal and professional experience, the "key" to working through the third step of recovery so that it is effective. *If you ignore this step out of fear or because you listened to others' opinions, your recovery won't work.* This step is the *most* important step of recovery.

Sometimes children understand the need to grieve and cry better than adults do. As I was writing this chapter, a friend e-mailed me a story about a four-year-old who understood something that many adults have forgotten.

> This child's next-door neighbor was an elderly gentleman who had recently lost his wife. Upon seeing the man cry, the little boy went into the old gentleman's yard, climbed onto his lap, and just sat there. When his mother asked what he had said to the neighbor, the little boy said, "Nothing, I just helped him cry!"

Your grieving may take the form of intense sadness, anger, and even rage. Don't act on these feelings other than to write them down. Don't be destructive to yourself or others, but let yourself feel these emotions. Grieve until you can't stand yourself anymore. I know I'm done with grieving something when I am sick of myself! Eventually you will go from feeling like you are carrying huge luggage with you every day of your life to being a light traveler who has discarded her baggage and is now feeling only intense relief.

The Expected Guilt

Guilt will rear its ugly head. Our culture teaches us that "good girls don't hate their mothers," so as you feel the anger, rage, and sadness, you can expect to feel guilt too. Let it be okay to feel guilt for right now. In nearly every interview and clinical session I have done with daughters of narcissistic mothers, the daughter will mention how bad she feels that she is talking negatively about her mother. It is a taboo that you must work through to get to the other side. I am not advocating that you hate her or express your anger to her. The rage will not last if you allow yourself to feel it now. You have to face your losses and disappointments before you can get past them. You are aiming to get past blame to that point of deeper understanding and peace within yourself. This will allow you to be at peace with your mother too.

- Martha, 62, tells me, "I had a guilt attack before this interview. My mother's favorite expression was, 'The bird shits in its own nest. Don't take it elsewhere.' She would be horrified and furious if she knew I had talked about her."

GRIEVING THE LOSS OF THE CHILD YOU DIDN'T GET TO BE

The next specific area of grief is grieving for the little "you" who didn't get to exist because you had to be an early caretaker for your mother, and sometimes for the whole family.

Think about what you might have been able to do if you had been allowed just to be a kid. Imagine yourself doing those things right now. Write them down and again look at what you missed out on. Let your feelings be there. Feel them. If you are artistic, draw some pictures of you doing those things you wanted to do. Maybe as an adult you can do them now. We will be discussing this more in chapter 12.

When I first worked through this stage of grief in my own recovery, I used an exercise that I often use with clients now. I would sit in a rocking chair after my children were in bed and rock, close my eyes, and imagine myself as a small child. I would get this visual of a little girl with long blond braids and red cowboy boots. I would then hold out my arms and ask her to come to me and tell me what she needed from me. At her first appearance, she was a sad, stomping, red-booted, angry kid, with flailing braids, but as she talked to me, I became aware that I had to take care of her now, and recognize what she had missed as a child. We would cry together in that rocking chair. I spent a lot of time doing this exercise repeatedly. Your inner kid will talk to you, too, if you invite her in. Write down in your journal what happens in each interaction.

Another technique that is helpful in getting in touch with your little-kid needs is what I call "doll therapy." Go shopping and find a little girl doll that resembles you between three and eight in age. Look until you find a doll you love, then bring her home and talk to her. Keep her on the bed, dresser, or couch so she is in plain sight to remind you that she has needs. Ask her what she has missed out on and what she needs from you now. Write down the thoughts that come up so that you don't lose them as you get busy in your day-to-day routines, which is easy to do. You want to be able to refer to the list to see where you still need to grieve and how to give yourself what you didn't get as a child.

As you engage in this grief process, allow the child or doll to speak to you at different ages. Allow her to go into her teen years, even up to age 18. Branded into many daughters' memories are the moments when they needed a mother to be there for them during the difficult teen years. If your memories begin to go even into your twenties or into adulthood, go with them. If you give yourself the quiet and the time, the feelings that you need to process will surface.

It is reasonable to seek a therapist for help during this part of your recovery. Try to follow the suggestions here on your own first, as they have been helpful in my sessions with daughters. But if you are stuck and nothing is coming to the surface, using professional help in the process can make a big difference. You may want to find a professional mental health provider who knows a technique called EMDR (Eye Movement Desensitization and Reprocessing), an area of expertise that is particularly helpful with processing feelings. Go to the emdria.org Web site to find an EMDR-qualified professional in your community. This Web site also provides articles on EMDR and helps you understand how the technique works. In short, it is a treatment that is designed to process trauma and desensitize the related emotions. Having used it for years with my clients, I can attest to its effectiveness. And it works more quickly than straight talk therapy.

Finding the right therapist means finding one with the proper qualifications and with whom you can connect personally—the key to a successful therapeutic experience. For this particular kind of therapeutic work, I even recommend a female therapist who is older than you are. It is also helpful if the therapist is a mother or grandmother. These are not absolutes, but helpful in establishing trust and emotional connectivity.

The most important aspect of the first steps of recovery for daughters of narcissistic mothers, however, is doing the acceptance and grief work on your own as much as you can, *before* moving on to the next chapters and suggestions. If you don't work on acceptance and grief, the rest of your recovery won't "take." You want to have a true and lasting recovery. If you think you have grappled with acceptance and grief, start on the next few chapters, and if you find they are not working for you, simply come back to these "first steps" and work them again. You want to—you have to!—clean this house first before you move along into emotional and spiritual home decorating.

- Lou, 44, tells me, "I have to admit, Dr. McBride, that I hated this part of the recovery, but, oh, was it worth it! I have tried over and over in my life to do the rest of the recovery you told me about and nothing seemed to work until I just broke down and felt this bad stuff!"

- Mimi says, "I have never seen myself as a raging, angry person. I always thought that meant I was being bitchy, and I avoided it like the plague. This step was very hard for me to do, especially the feelings part. I could talk up a storm about my mother, but I never wanted to admit to myself that she had hurt me so much. It was like she won again and I was once again a victim. I see now that I had to be this raging, bitchy victim to get to the other side."

The other side is where you will begin to grow and sustain yourself. When you're ready, join me in doing that in the next chapter.

CHAPTER ELEVEN

A Part Of and Apart From

SEPARATING FROM MOTHER

> Because if everyone just turns out like their mother, then
> what's the rat's ass point?
> —Elizabeth Strout, *Amy and Isabelle*[1]

To become authentic and whole—this is the ultimate goal in recovering from a narcissistic mother. The next step for you to take toward this is to separate psychologically from Mother as an adult, so that you can grow your own internal emotional psyche. For when you grow your internal emotional being, you become resilient and strong. You can stand on your own. You can sustain yourself in the face of maternal deprivation, bear up under any negative litanies from your mother, and withstand criticism from anyone in the external environment. You will become a woman who can be around your mother and be away from her, and you will remain whole in both situations. This is the ability to be *a part of and apart from* at the same time, all the while keeping in steady access a solid sense of self.

Why Is Psychological Separation from Mother Important for Your Mental Health?

Individuation, a normal part of development, begins at about age two as a child begins to say "no" and "mine," and continues throughout life as the child matures, develops her own wants, needs, and desires, and deliberately breaks away from her parents to form a healthy sense of self. Healthy parents allow this to happen gradually and naturally.

The individuation process is stunted for children of a narcissistic mother, because she has either engulfed or ignored them. An ignored child does not get her emotional needs met and cannot work on self and separation because she is still trying to fill up her own tank with Mother's love. She keeps trying to merge with her mother like a small infant, trying to get Mother's approval and attention. An engulfed child is discouraged from seeing herself as separate from her mother and from having individual needs, desires, thoughts, or feelings. Neither daughter's emotional needs are met and each has difficulty in developing a sense of self. If you've grappled with issues of control over your own life and feelings, or you can't enjoy your successes, you are struggling, like most daughters of narcissistic mothers, to separate and individuate. You are probably still searching for and developing the whole you.

For many years, at the times I felt overwhelmed, I had a favorite saying: "I'm too little for that." I would find myself using it whenever I faced a big project or was up against a major life decision. One day it dawned on me that this was an unconscious expression of a much deeper reality. During a therapy session, while I was processing the breakup of a love relationship, my therapist innocently asked me why I had decided to stay in the house in which I'd lived with the man I was getting over. It seemed too big for just one person, so why did I not move and find my own smaller, more practical home that could be "just mine"? I remember feeling blank and numb, and responded, "I'm too little to move." My therapist's eyes glistened, and he smiled. I felt instantly defensive and annoyed, but he gently explained, "That's the issue right there."

I did feel "too little." When you haven't completed individuation with your mother, it leaves you unfinished and emotionally immature, a half person aspiring to become a whole person. If your emotional self has been stunted, it doesn't grow in proportion to your physical, intellectual, and spiritual self. You have to heal in order to become whole.

Years ago, in times of stress, I would unconsciously recite the words "Oh, Mommy." Thank goodness that impulse is gone, but I do remember how infantile and orphaned I felt. It makes me smile to write this today simply because I can acknowledge this and be grateful that I have grown beyond it.

Part of separating from your mother and childhood is ridding yourself of negative self-talk, such as, "I'm not good enough," "I'm unlovable," "I can't trust myself." Because you have internalized these messages, they speak to you now as your mother once did. Decide for yourself what those messages say, block them out, and override them. As you do this, you separate in a healthy way from your dysfunctional mother and her self-defeating belief system. You will recognize yourself as an individual woman.

- Gracie, 35, remembers her struggle to individuate with painful clarity. "It took me a long time to feel like a separate person from my mother. She merged into me and then it was all about her—no distance."

- Marianne wants to be close to her family, but needs to maintain her hard-won sense of self. "I seem to do really well with my established sense of self until I get around my mother and the family and then it's like I get sucked back into the old roles we all used to play. I want so badly to just be me even when I am around all of them."

What Does Separation Mean, Exactly?

Psychological literature explains separation-individuation as defining a sense of self and as differentiation. Every person has to undertake individuation from her family of origin to grow up fully. Psychological separation is an internal process and has nothing to do with geo-graphically separating from your mother or family of origin. According to renowned family therapist Dr. Murray Bowen, an adult can regard herself to be further along with her individuation process the more she (1) becomes less emotionally reactive to the family dynamics, (2) becomes more objective in observing the family dynamics, and (3) becomes aware of the "myths, images, distortions, and triangles" she had been blind to while growing up.[2] As you undergo the acceptance and grief processes in the previous chapter, you can undertake these steps successfully. As Bowen states:

> The person who acquires a little ability at becoming an observer and at controlling some of his emotional reactiveness acquires an ability that is useful for life in all kinds of emotional snarls. Most of the time he can live his life, reacting with appropriate and natural emotional responses, but with the knowledge that at any time he can back out of the situation, slow down his reactiveness, and make observations that help him control himself and the situation.[3]

How Do I Release Myself from the Mother Orbit?

Releasing yourself from orbiting around your mother is the only way to gain true mastery over your life choices and to become who you are meant to be. I take my clients through the following three steps when they are moving through this stage of development: (1) understand how your mother projects feelings onto you; (2) understand and cope with envy from your mother and others; and (3) eradicate negative internalized messages. Let's go through them together on the following pages.

PROJECTION

Projection is best understood as a process by which a person takes her own emotions and sees them as coming from someone else, believing that the other person actually originated those emotions. People do this when they are not dealing with their own pain or inner conflicts and blame other people for their own turmoil. Daughters of narcissistic mothers are generally the scapegoats for their mothers' projections, including fragile ego and self-loathing. The daughter doesn't understand this hatred and internalizes it so that she feels that she is bad or not good enough. Because this begins for the daughter at such a young age, it feels normal and real.

COPING WITH MOTHER'S ENVY

Daughters of narcissistic mothers commonly feel their mothers' envy. It's time to recognize and understand it. Many people believe that to be envied would be a desirable, powerful experience, but in reality being envied, particularly by one's own mother, is unnerving and awful. The daughter's sense of self is canceled by disdain and criticism. Her goodness is questioned or labeled bad or made light of, which causes her to feel like "her reality as a person is obliterated."[4] As the daughter analyzes what her mother appears jealous about—her looks, achievements, material wealth, weight, personality, friends, husband or boyfriend, or relationship with her father or siblings—she comes to feel unworthy. It makes no sense to the daughter that her own mother would have these bad feelings about her, and therefore she believes something is wrong with her.

Daughters typically have a difficult time coming to terms with being envied and being able to discuss it openly. I believe this is because they don't want to appear arrogant in even thinking that someone could envy them. We can discuss our being jealous of someone or something, but to say we think someone is envious of us sounds haughty, eh? Daughters of narcissistic mothers usually do not see their own goodness enough to recognize envy for what it is, but believe they have done something wrong once again. Well, for you this envy was very real, particularly if you can recall specific comments, criticisms, and judgments your mother made about you or about things you did. You might have tried to make sense of them before, but it is important for you now to write down any comments that felt like envy. Seeing them in black and white in your journal will help you recognize the distortions that came your way and created an awful feeling inside your very soul.

If you blamed yourself for these comments and tried to right what seemed to you to be a misunderstanding, your efforts no doubt failed, for it is impossible to mend a narcissist's distorted sense of envy. Envy just allows the insecure mother to feel temporarily better about herself. When she envies and then criticizes and devalues you, she cancels you out of her life and in this way diminishes the threat to her fragile self-esteem. Envy is a powerful tool in the narcissist's repertoire, and you have likely seen it in your mother's interactions with other people. When she directs it at you, however, it creates a feeling of helplessness and painful self-doubt.

To release yourself from your confusion and see the envy for what it is, recognize your own goodness and strength. Do not be spiteful or retaliate with ugliness. The envy that is thrown your way does not belong to you, and you do not have to identify with it. You can be real and feel the hurt and the sadness but not attack back or seek revenge. Hang on to the good that is within you. Most daughters I have worked with are not vengeful, so you most likely are not either. Is it any wonder that Cinderella is the favorite fairy tale mentioned by daughters of narcissistic mothers?

ERADICATING NEGATIVE MESSAGES

To rid yourself of negative messages, first think about how you make a wide range of decisions. Do you base your choices on information that you trust? Is that information usually from a reliable source? Do you typically have data that tell you that this source is someone on whom you can rely, someone with the credentials to be giving you advice or assistance? Have you generally had a good experience with this person and been able to trust his or her perceptions, information, and knowledge? Does this reliable source mostly treat you with respect and care about how you feel? Most likely your answer to each of these questions is yes.

I ask you, then, Is it wise to take those internalized messages from childhood and believe them, since they came from someone who was not authentic, loving, or empathetic, who could not establish an intimate emotional bond with you, who projected her own feelings onto you, as she was not in touch with her own emotions, and who was also envious of you? Why would you allow this person to define who you are? Consider the source. Remind yourself of this as you take a pen or go to a computer and identify and record those negative messages. Write them down in one column, and in another column, write about why they are simply not true. In doing so, you are redefining what you believe to be true about yourself. Is it really true, for example, that you are not good enough? Who says? You only have to be good enough for you!

Once you have identified the negative messages and have answered back, saying why they are not correct, your next task is to remember to do this same exercise whenever a message pops up in your mind. This way you will erase the old and put in the new—each time one appears in your mind. It will take some practice, but eventually your persistence will pay off.

Even though working this recovery program will bring you success, if you have difficulty getting rid of your internalized messages and need additional assistance, this is another time in your recovery that a therapist using Eye Movement Desensitization and Reprocessing (EMDR) could help you. You would take your specific negative messages to your therapist, who will likely ask you to put a traumatic memory with each message for the EMDR therapy to be effective.

The Separation Criteria

How do you know when your real self has developed and has separated from orbiting with Mother? How do you know when you have successfully uncoupled from maternal dysfunction and are truly standing tall, strong, and able? James Masterson, in *The Search for the Real Self*, describes the key capacities of the real self.[5] I have interpreted for daughters, below:

- *The capacity to experience a wide range of feelings deeply with liveliness, joy, vigor, excitement, and spontaneity.* You allow yourself to feel your authentic feelings and do not create barriers to numb the full gamut of human emotion. You allow yourself to express these feelings in appropriate ways.

- *The capacity to expect appropriate entitlements.* You believe in yourself, and are no longer filled with the angst of self-doubt, so you are freely giving yourself credit where credit is due.

- *The capacity for self-activation and assertion.* You can identify your dreams and desires and are able to set out to accomplish them while believing you can do it.

- *The acknowledgment of self-esteem.* You now believe you are worthy and can validate yourself regardless of external, worldly approval.

- *The ability to soothe painful feelings.* When life creates painful situations, you can comfort yourself, not wallow in misery, and can find solutions.

- *The ability to make and stick to commitments.* When decisions are right for you, you can stick to your guns and overcome obstacles, criticism, and setbacks.

- *Creativity.* You can find solutions to problems and be resourceful and also replace and defuse negatives with positives.

- *Intimacy.* You can express yourself fully and honestly in a close relationship with another person with minimal anxiety about abandonment or engulfment. You can create emotional intimacy without fear or anxiety about being abandoned or swallowed up.

- *The ability to be alone.* You can enjoy a relationship with yourself, be alone, and find meaning within.

- *Continuity of self.* Your inner core is real and remains the same through the trials and tribulations of life, and throughout the aging process.

You may be thinking, Sounds good, but I can never get there! The remaining chapters will assist you in accomplishing all of the above. Remember, however, recovery is lifelong work and you cannot accomplish all of them at once. Here are some encouraging stories of women who have individuated from their mothers.

- "I never understood the 'individuation process' until I began to undergo therapy. Now I can see her and keep me at the same time. I cannot tell you how much this means to me" (Erin, 40).

- "Understanding the envy part was a big step for me. This has been a painful thing in my life forever—my mother, sister, and some female friends showed envy and I always had to keep a tight lid on anything good or successful I was doing because I didn't want to get their wrath. Now I understand it has nothing to do with me and I am able to be proud of myself and give myself credit. I can't tell you how important this has been to my belief in myself. I always had to disparage myself to feel accepted and now I can just be me" (Annabel, 34).

- "It always seemed like if I made mistakes, I was more accepted by my mother. When I did well, she always had something bad to say. Or she would make comments about me getting too high on myself. This hurt so much. Now it doesn't matter really what she says. I have worked so hard on individuating from her because I now know that she is not a reliable source to define me anymore. This finally makes sense" (Chloe, 62).

- Holly, whose mother is a minister, has forever felt pressured and "less than" because she did not choose her family's religion as an adult. "After doing this recovery work, I find that when my mother sends me letters with scripture about what kind of wife I should be, I no longer ruminate for days and become undone. I am able to accept her beliefs as hers and also accept my own separate beliefs about my spirituality and lifestyle. It feels so neutral now. Like I am in control of my life."

- "I used to cry for days after just talking to my mother on the phone. She always gave me messages about how I would never quite measure up and I took it so personally. Now I can see that she is not a reliable source. She has some serious problems that she has always put onto me. I still think this is so very sad and it sucks, but I no longer take it on" (Josette, 39).

Let's move on to the next chapter, so we can focus more on you and your unique qualities as a truly deserving woman.

CHAPTER TWELVE

BECOMING THE WOMAN I TRULY AM

DESERVING DAUGHTERS

It is not easy to find happiness in ourselves, and it is not possible to find it elsewhere.

—Agnes Repplier,
The Treasure Chest[1]

After years of having been coerced into being what your mother wanted you to be—whether it was how you looked and acted, or what you believed in and valued—it is time now to focus on what you want for yourself. No more succumbing to Mother's attempt to mold you into her image. No more putting your internal growth on hold in order to please Mom. No more superficial smiles on pretty little faces.

In order to do the fun work I encourage in this chapter, I want you to address two serious issues.

- How to erect and strengthen your "internal mother"
- How to understand and manage "the collapse"[2]

Below, we will take each concept in turn and discuss the strategies you need to recover.

The Internal Mother

The internal mother is best understood as your own maternal instinct. It is the intuitive voice that speaks to you and wants to nurture, love, and mother you. While in the past you had to give up on the notion that your external mother could give you what you needed, you can now have an internal mother readily available to you. She makes it possible to parent yourself.

Many daughters are sad and angry when first confronted with the concept of parenting themselves, but when they realize and accept these feelings, they get through them to a sense of inner strength and empowerment.

To grow the internal mother, you must first give her permission to be there. You allow her kind, maternal voice to resonate within you. You allow yourself to hear it. To begin, find a quiet, lovely healing place where you will have solitude. This may be the bathtub, your deck, office, or on a walk. Whatever works for you. Try to create an atmosphere where you will not be interrupted. After you've done this several times, you will be able to do this anywhere and even go through interruptions. But start with having complete quiet and focusing on yourself. Have your journal, writing pad, and pencil with you.

Your first task is making what I call the "I am" list. To do this, it is important to allow your internal mother to share and review your many incredible strengths and characteristics. Write them down in a manner similar to these examples:

"I am strong, I am intelligent, I am wise, I am loving, I am helpful, I am empathetic, I am industrious, I am energetic, I am productive, I am sensitive, I am honest, I am a person with integrity, I am talented, I am caring, I am responsible, I am spiritual, I am beautiful inside and out, I am healthy."

Your next task is to push away negative messages like "I don't have any good traits." You know in your heart that you do. If you give her permission, your internal mother will help validate and verify the positive *you* sitting right there. If the negative thoughts persist, it is a red flag that you have additional grieving and trauma to process and you must go back to first steps. As discussed earlier, reaffirming messages do not "stick" unless you have done the proper grieving.

Your "I am" list is the starting point with your internal mother. Practice being with her. Talk to her often and let her console you. I often tell clients to treat themselves at this point as they would treat a two-year-old child. Be gentle, kind, understanding, and sweet. You so deserve this. When you don't know what to do, ask yourself how your own maternal self would treat a child with this same emotion or struggle and then do that. When I think of two-year-olds, I think about scooping them up and giving them lots of love and attention. I bet your maternal instinct is similar.

As you practice conferring with your internal mother, she will begin to grow and strengthen. You will feel a committee forming of "me, myself, and I." The internal mother heads this association. I have found that the times to practice and strengthen the internal mother are in those situations where you want to reach out for help and advice from someone else because you don't know what to do. This is the time to go internally and find intuitive answers and consolation from the maternal committee. The more that you confer with them, the stronger and more self-assured you become. This mother will never abandon you.

You will particularly need the internal mother when you experience what is called "the collapse."

The Collapse

In true narcissism, the narcissist often experiences something called a "narcissistic injury." According to the *Diagnostic and Statistical Manual of Mental Disorders (DSM)*:

> Vulnerability in self-esteem makes individuals with narcissistic personality disorder very sensitive to "injury" from criticism or

defeat. Although they may not show it outwardly, criticism may haunt these individuals and may leave them feeling humiliated, degraded, hollow and empty. They may react with disdain, rage, or defiant counterattack.[3]

The narcissistic individuals I have known who have had this kind of injury reaction take a long time to get over it; they hold grudges, want to get back at the person they perceived harmed them; they seek revenge, try to cause problems for their attacker, and seem never to forget or forgive. Most daughters of narcissistic mothers with whom I have worked experience a similar condition, although to a much lesser degree, which is called "the collapse." They feel as if they just popped their self-esteem balloon and all the air rushed out and they need a bit of time to restabilize and refill that balloon. It is different from the narcissist's injury, because it doesn't last long and the daughter is able to forgive and forget, and she is not haunted or humiliated for long periods of time. She is also typically not out to get revenge, do paybacks, or seek to harm. The daughter's collapse is due to her internal sensitivity caused by being insulted and invalidated as a child, adolescent, and adult by her narcissistic mother. When it happens during recovery, it is as if it triggers a momentary regression back to childhood; old memories make the current situation feel much bigger than it really is. This "domino effect" leads to the feeling of internal "collapse," which is also described as a result of post-traumatic stress disorder, commonly referred to as PTSD. The *DSM* explains this further:

> The traumatic event is persistently reexperienced in one or more of the following ways. . . . Intense psychological distress at exposure to internal or external cues that symbolize or resemble an aspect of the traumatic event, and . . . physiological reactivity on exposure to internal or external cues that symbolize or resemble an aspect of the traumatic event.[4]

This means that the daughter will feel the collapse when something reminds her of early childhood wounds. At this moment, a daughter is most tempted to reach out for external validation and ask someone else to make it better for her, and she may act needy. You can manage this differently—without acting needy—by going to your internal mother for support and comfort.

Without naming it, daughters frequently describe "the collapse." As Felicity told me:

- I was recently sitting with a guest at my house who announced to me that he was having one of his employees stop by my house to pick up a work check. I thought this was a bit strange, but certainly okay with me. The employee did stop by, and I welcomed her into my house and offered her a beverage while chatting briefly. We had never met before. When she left, after only about ten minutes, I walked her to the door, and expressed that it was nice to meet her. She responded with "Nice to meet you too, even though you have issues." I was floored by this inappropriate comment from someone who didn't even know me. I knew instinctively that it was about something that was going on with her, but it still felt like a punch in the stomach, and that feeling lasted for a whole damn day! Why, Dr. McBride, would I allow this stranger's inappropriate comment to bother me so?

As in the past with her mother, Felicity was reminded of years she had tried to be so good and pleasing, to do things right and be kind and polite and then got zapped in the end as never being good enough. This domino effect or collapse took Felicity back to historical wounds, but she handled it by talking to me, her therapist, and a friend. She reached out for external validation in this case, but eventually learned to manage other situations like this on her own, which was her recovery.

Now that you are aware of what the collapse is, you will be better prepared to deal with it when it happens to you. Notice your reactions in the next week; keep track of how many times a collapse actually happens to you. Your increasing awareness will give you increasing strength. You are in charge of you.

Kristal describes another example of a collapse moment:

- I stopped by my friend's house to see if she could babysit for a couple of hours while I ran some errands. We do this for each other often and we are both fine with it. On this particular day, however, my friend, Beth, asked me how long I would be gone because she had laundry to do. That was it. She just set a boundary and asked a simple question, but I immediately interpreted it as her intimating that I was being a burden on her, and she did not want to help me.

In Kristal's case, the friend had good boundaries, but what she asked, although not inappropriate, triggered in Kristal feelings of being a burden on her mother, and she had a strong reaction that lasted for several days.

The collapse can cause another problem, as described by Joanie, 36.

- We were at a family barbecue and I was sparring with my brother. We do this a lot, but on this day, he actually told me I had gained too much weight and my butt looked big. He always teases me about trying to look "J-Lo-ish," his term for a great-looking butt and body. But today, he just said, "Big!" I was hurt. I went to my sister and complained to her, and she said, "Why would you let him bother you? He's just a brat, and who cares what anybody says about your butt? Get over it." Then, I was not only hurt by my brother, but mad at my sister for not supporting me and giving me sympathy. The thing that bothers me most, though, is that I thought about it for a week and it reminded me so much of the constant criticism and insults from Mom about my weight while growing up.

Joanie's experience with her weeklong collapse is interesting. First she was *hurt* and then *angry* at not being rescued from her pain. She could have worked on this and shortened her distress if she had strengthened and called on her internal mother, who could have comforted her immediately. Instead, she did not get the validation for her feelings that she needed until she came to therapy a week later. Again, getting support is a good thing, and we all need it on occasion, but you can save a week of feeling bad by building up your self-reliance—your internal mother.

The Sensitive One

Daughters were often called "the sensitive one" in the family. They tire of people telling them that they are overreacting to things said or done by other people. Daughters of narcissistic mothers have to work on freeing themselves of this tie to their past. You will feel more normal and less crazy when you understand that any temporary collapse is a normal reaction to a trigger from your history. When you can identify and understand it, you can also work to relieve it and prevent it from recurring. Otherwise, you may tend to beat up on yourself for letting things bother you and buying into the old "you're the sensitive one" script.

- Deadra, 35, tells me, "Feelings were generally not allowed in our family, so whenever I had some feeling going on and tried to express it, I was told that I was being too sensitive. That usually shut me down, but I didn't know what to do with the feelings that were left inside of me."

- Melodie, 42, said, "I'm so sick of people telling me I'm oversensitive! My mother said that to me anytime I showed even one little feeling growing up. I know it is because she couldn't deal with my feelings and so she wouldn't allow them. Now, when my husband or children say the same to me, I just want to bop them. I want to be real and have whatever feelings I have and quit worrying about it."

Now that you understand why you need to strengthen the internal mother and recognize your being at risk for periodic emotional collapses, you are ready to start reinventing yourself. After the painful work of prior chapters, the rest of this chapter should be fun and entertaining. For the exercises that follow, you need only your own approval and that of your internal mother, who is always on your side, no matter what. Let's get started, so you can discover your passions and preferences, which you may have kept under wraps before now, when it was "all about Mom." You will be asking yourself questions such as:

- What do I value most?
- What makes me happy?
- What gives me the deepest sense of fulfillment?
- What are my passions and talents?

Who Am I Really?

Because daughters of narcissistic mothers have been forced into supporting roles demanded by their mothers and the narcissistic family system, it is not uncommon for them to say they don't really know who they are or what they like. They have become accustomed to doing for others and not focusing on themselves in healthy ways. As Mei tells me, "The message I got from Mom is that she will love me if I do what she thinks I should do. So I try to be me, but I don't know who I am."

To begin the discovery process, it is important to know the basics of what you like and what you believe in. To do this, I am going to suggest two exercises to get you started.

Real-Woman Collage

Although not new or innovative, this exercise is helpful for women beginning to think about themselves in a different way. To do this exercise, get a poster board or piece of construction paper and several women's magazines. Start thumbing through the magazines to find pictures of women who represent womanhood to you. Pay attention to what you choose: Are the images representing what you really desire or what your mother or someone else thinks you should be? Cut out only those images or pictures that represent what you believe are symbols of positive, adult womanhood to you, representations of who you are and who you want to become when you allow yourself to show forth. When you have found images that fit you, make a collage of them on the paper. Keep this collage as a reminder of where you are going with your re-creation or finding of yourself.

What Are My Values?

This exercise assists you in reminding yourself what you believe in and determining what you like. You will make a list of beliefs on your desires and preferences. I will give you my starting list, and you can add to it as you think of beliefs on which you want to focus. The categories will be a combination of simple, seemingly unimportant things and huge, significant life philosophies. For each category, it is your job to write what is your style, preference or belief.

- Education: your beliefs and philosophy about education for yourself and your family
- Politics: your political beliefs

- Religion: your religious or spiritual beliefs
- Parenting belief system: How do you want to raise your children and what are your priorities as a mother?
- Love relationship: What are the most important things to you in a love relationship?
- Men: Who is the ideal man for you; what are his characteristics?
- Friends: What kind of friends are you attracted to?
- Movies: What kind of movies do you like best?
- Books: What kind of books are your favorites?
- Jewelry: What is your style of jewelry?
- Fashion: What is your style of clothing?
- Cars: If you could buy whatever cars you wanted, which two would you choose?
- Architecture and house style: What kind of architecture do you like?
- Furniture: What are your favorite kinds of furniture?
- Gemstone: your favorite gemstones
- Weather: your favorite weather
- Geography: your favorite landscape
- Season: Which of the seasons is your favorite and why?
- Music for listening: What kind of music do you like for pure listening and pleasure?
- Music for dancing: What is your favorite dance music?
- Leisure-time activity: What leisure-time activity do you like most?
- Kick-up-your-heels fun: What activity do you love that brings you sheer joy?
- Exercise: your favorite kind of exercise
- Television show: What do you like to watch on television?
- Food: your favorite foods to cook and eat
- Restaurant: When you dine out, where do you most like to go?
- Shopping place: What is your favorite shopping place?

- Vacation: your ideal vacation
- Sports to play: If you play sports, which do you enjoy most?
- Sports to watch: If you watch sports, what is your favorite?
- Color: What is your favorite color for wearing and decorating?
- Fabrics: What is your favorite fabric for wearing and decorating?
- Flowers: your favorite flowers
- Conversation: your favorite kind of conversation; about what and with whom?
- Favorite age group: What age group do you most like to hang out with?

Add more as you go. The purpose here is to be writing and thinking about yourself through your thoughts, desires, preferences, beliefs, and values. We rarely take time to stop and ask ourselves these kinds of questions, and you will be surprised at how much "self" you already have and how much you do really know about you.

If I Were Good Enough

The next exercise can be very helpful if you spend time on it and think carefully about it. At the top of a page in your journal, you write the heading "If I Were Good Enough." Then write about the things you would do if you felt good enough right now. "If I were good enough, I would _____." Keep at this until you have written at least ten things. I'm always surprised when I do this myself, as I find it can change from year to year. It is also a useful way to demonstrate that you have vanquished the old negative internal messages and that they are not controlling your choices any longer.

After doing this exercise, read it to someone who loves you and get his or her reaction. Allow your internal mother to digest it as well. Then start doing the things on that list.

Finding Your Interests in a Memory Exercise

It worries me when I ask women what they are interested in and they say they don't know. If this is the case for you, I want you to take some quiet time to think about what you liked to do as a small child. What kinds of things did you play with? Sometimes you can take a childhood activity and transfer it to an adult activity that fits your current interests beautifully. For example, when I did this, I remembered that before I turned seven, we lived in the country and rode Shetland ponies. I loved the horses and the countryside, but they also reminded me of country dancing and country music and I threw myself into those activities again. They are two of my favorite pastimes now. I also used to love to play paper dolls, which translates into a love of clothes and fashion today. Try this remembering exercise and see what you come up with.

Perhaps you are aware of what interests you have but do not allow yourself the time to explore them or experience fun. To get in touch with the real you, you have to involve the child side of you to laugh and have a really good time. Don't deny this core part of you any longer. Find what it is for you. Allow yourself both leisure-time enjoyment and what I call "kick up your heels" kind of fun. An example of these two different activities for me would be attending a spectacular musical, which I would find very enjoyable, versus dancing with a great dancer to my favorite music, which would be "kick up your heels" fun. You may love rock climbing for three days in the wilderness, but your girlfriend may prefer a Ritz-Carlton kind of vacation. Find out what constitutes pleasure and enjoyment and what is out-of-control, belly-laughing fun for you.

When you do figure out your specific interests, then it is time to set up your schedule to include them in your life. You may suddenly be taking piano lessons or dance lessons or ski lessons. A client of mine recently started belly dancing and loves it—it's great exercise and she laughs and has fun. Her husband likes it, too, when she has to practice at home. You may find that you want to explore some new things but have no one to do it with. If this is the case, it is important to make yourself do them alone. Going to movies, dancing, hiking, walking—whatever it is—do it alone. The time you spend with yourself is very important in improving your self-understanding and self-reliance. Time alone may seem like a luxury, but I assure you that this time spent on your own interests is very important to your recovery.

Your age should never be a factor. I am working with several women in their fifties, sixties, and seventies who are just now getting to do things they always wanted to do and are finding great joy.

Keep a list of the true interests you discover in your recovery journal. It helps to refer back to them and take encouragement from this aspect of your recovery whenever you find that you also have to do some painful processing. Recovery can have a fun side—in fact, it has to—so be sure to include this part. Being nice to yourself is a gift that you and your internal mother can provide regularly and reliably, as no one else can. Give permission! Don't allow yourself to get caught up in believing that taking care of yourself and enjoying yourself is selfish. On the contrary, it is a vital, necessary part of your recovery.

Actually, Let's Talk About Selfish

Many daughters in recovery have been taught by their narcissistic mothers and our patriarchal culture that focusing on their own needs is selfish. Women are the primary "caretakers" of others and are asked to be in a giving mode at all times. And daughters of narcissistic mothers have also been treated as if they were not worthy of loving care. But, remember, you can't give what you don't have. People who are fulfilled have an overflow of love and energy and therefore can give freely of themselves to others without becoming exhausted. Their own tanks are full and charged, and they have energy to spare. If your spirit and energy are chronically depleted, if you are unhappy and unfulfilled, you will find it difficult to care for others. Thomas J. Leonard, personal coach and founder of Coach University, said it best:

Creativity and excellence require selfishness. So does evolution. When you know you're onto something—a potential breakthrough of any kind—you need the purest kind of focus and concentration possible. You need to answer to the callings of your heart and mind before you answer to the callings of the tribe. You need to accept that a reasonable and responsible level of selfishness builds long-term benefits for everyone you care about.[5]

Physical Health

Although I am not a medical doctor, this chapter would not be complete without mentioning the importance of your physical health. Because some daughters are at risk for sabotaging themselves and engaging in self-destructive behaviors, I want you to accept fully that taking good care of your health is mandatory. Sound mental health and recovery is not possible without your physical well-being. I will list only general health areas to make sure that you include these in your recovery plan. If you are not attending to one or more entries in the list below, ask yourself why and figure out the barrier so that you can overcome it. If you are having difficulty with something like an addiction, find an additional recovery program to enter so that you are getting the help you need. I compiled the following list after consulting with family practice physician James Gregory, M.D.[6]

- Have a complete physical examination that includes a thorough history and set up an individual health plan with general testing related to your age requirements. Some examples are: a colonoscopy after age 50 and a bone density test after age 60.
- Eat a balanced, nutritious diet.
- Drink plenty of water (48 ounces of water daily, by eight-ounce glass).
- Exercise regularly for at least 30 minutes, three times a week or more often. Include resistance training, e.g., weightlifting,

in order to preserve bone density as well as aerobic exercise for general health.

- Get regular dental examinations and cleanings twice a year.
- Get adequate sleep at night. The amount of sleep varies with individual needs, but most physicians now recommend seven to eight hours a night. If you are tired, it means you need more. If you have good energy throughout the day, you are probably getting enough.
- Address problems of excessive consumption. Eating too much, smoking, taking drugs, and drinking alcohol to excess are, of course, detrimental to long-term health.

Talent Search

The next area to assess is your talent. We are all born with some innate talent. It is your job to figure out what that talent is and pursue it if you desire. I have talked to many daughters of narcissistic mothers who are wildly talented in some area but have never pursued their talent because they do not believe in themselves. Some daughters are very aware of their talents because their mothers pushed them like showbiz moms, but are now burned out and not using what they know and can do. Others were never encouraged.

If you have a special gift and want to use it, pursue it, and try it again, do so. Work on grieving and healing any memories connected with your mother that are preventing you from following your talent, reconnecting with it, picking it up again. Life is short and you were given certain aptitudes for a reason. You don't have to be a superstar. Whatever you do will be good enough. This exercise is not meant for anyone else. This is for you! One daughter I worked with, a talented artist, did not want to paint and sell or start her own gallery, but she did want to use her talent. She ended up volunteering in art classes at her neighborhood school and loved it. Another daughter had a beautiful singing voice and started singing in the church choir. You can be very creative with how you use your talents. Allow the full you to be in operation now.

Indulge Your Passions

Not everyone has a passion, but if you do, don't let this world go by without at least trying your hand at whatever brings you deep excitement and purpose. You must explore the things that stir your soul. You do not have to be the best at anything. You can strive to be the best if you choose to, but it is your choice now. You are good enough to try to do whatever you want. You are driving the bus of your own life journey.

My passion is dance. I have dabbled in it for years and dance whenever I can. When I finish writing this book, I plan to explore every avenue of dance I can. This passion will take me into retirement doing something I dearly love. That's what I hope for you too.

Sit with your journal now and write about anything that brings you life and excitement. What is your deep personal interest and desire? Make yourself get in touch with a passion even if you feel like you don't have one. Your passion can be something with social significance, something that helps others, or it can be something that is just for you—something you like to collect, read, cook, or track; sewing, scrapbooking, quilting, climbing, hiking—whatever.

Hopefully, by doing the exercises offered in this chapter, you are further along in answering the important questions we started with:

- What do I value most?
- What makes me happy?
- What gives me the deepest sense of fulfillment?
- What are my passions and talents?

You have learned to strengthen your internal mother in order to build your self-confidence and to become more self-reliant. You now know how to deal with "the collapse" and get beyond these setbacks.

I hope you are feeling more positive about yourself and can relate to Amy, who says:

- "My experience and my character are my gifts. I am a quirky chick now, but a very positive person. My life is my choice and I accept responsibility for my actions."

My client Bonnie said,

- "I used to not be able to love myself; there was a dichotomy between what I knew and what I felt. I can feel that love for myself now and I am a free woman, finally!"

You, too, gained the skills you need to build new internal strength. Now we move into the process of managing your relationship with your actual mother in a healthy, new manner.

CHAPTER THIRTEEN

My Turn

DEALING WITH MOTHER DURING RECOVERY

> Their mothers may be long dead or white-haired, and in-
> firm, but still they have a profound hold on their daugh-
> ters, who talk of them as though they were about to be
> sent to their rooms. How is this reign of terror by little old
> ladies possible?
>
> —Victoria Secunda,
> *When You and Your Mother Can't Be Friends*[1]

You have earned the right to be proud of yourself for a number
of reasons, not least of which is all the self-healing work that
you have accomplished. Now let's figure out what to do about your
mother if she is still around, still a part of your life in some way.
You've changed, and she hasn't. At this stage in your recovery, you
must explore ways for you to manage your relationship with her and
remain healthy yourself.

Even though you are feeling stronger and have a more solid sense
of self, you probably approach decisions about how to cope with
Mother with trepidation. You might be asking yourself the following: "What can I say to her?" "Can she be fixed?" "How do I deal
with her?" "Should I stay connected with her even though it is extremely difficult and painful for me?" Many daughters have tried
various ways to avoid the train wrecks they go through with their

narcissistic mothers. Frequently, though, they hit barriers, problems, and frustrations.

- Virginia keeps trying, although she is ambivalent. Her current strategy is to call it like she sees it. By doing this, she hopes things will improve. "I am always fighting with her. I am a lot more confrontational with her than I ever was before. I don't care what she says. I am more critical of her now. I call her a liar. I still have that hope that maybe I can fix it. If I give her enough evidence, maybe I could break through her barrier. Maybe I could help her. I'm so uncertain as to how it will turn out now."

- Nakia doesn't want to change the way she deals with her mother. "I have been dealing with this situation for most of my life, and she has never gotten better. I have not gone for the 'big confrontation,' as she is 83 and I don't want to ruin her remaining years. Our limited relationship for the past 15 years has been all about her—that seems to be the only way."

- Belva has little energy left for hope. "She is always baiting me and she loves to rile me up. It makes her happy and powerful to see me diminished. It leaves me exhausted and empty, and I don't believe there is a solution."

- Teri recalls, "Sometimes I get so afraid of having to talk to her on the telephone, I have to psych myself up for it. A glass of wine also helps! I never know what she is going to say. I mean this woman criticizes trees! Always negative."

In this chapter, I offer suggestions on how to manage these difficult situations. It can be frustrating to figure out the healthy path to take with a narcissistic mother. It is a significant struggle, one that appears to leave many daughters feeling hopeless, helpless, and in pain. So, what can you do?

The Untreatables

If your mother has a full-blown narcissistic personality disorder (NPD), the chances of effective treatment for her, or change, are slight. While I would never say it's impossible, it would require intensive, long-term, committed treatment, and most important, her desire to be treated. It is quite rare for a person with true NPD to seek therapy for herself and to genuinely want to change and grow personally. In my experience, NPD clients who do seek therapy are searching for answers in how to deal with someone else. If they do express a desire to work on themselves, they drop out of therapy rather quickly, usually telling me that they need to find a therapist with a different approach. Typically, in their eyes, there is something wrong with me, the therapist.

My favorite story is from a few years back when my therapy fee was $100 per session. In the midst of my explaining what constitutes good mother-daughter communication, this rather aggressive mother began searching frantically in her purse. She then dragged out a $100 bill along with her cigarette lighter and proceeded to light the bill on fire, saying, "This is what I think of your therapy advice!" I had to laugh. Thankfully, the daughter and I put out the fire and ended that infamous mother-daughter session quickly.

The more traits your mother has that fit the disorder, the less likely she is a candidate for successful treatment. This means that you can't fix her and should not be attempting it. Since she is not going to change, you may then ask whether or not you should continue to have contact with her, particularly if her behavior causes you significant emotional distress.

Toxic Mothers

We have to acknowledge that a narcissistic mother may be too toxic to be around. In many situations, daughters have to make the choice to disconnect completely from their mothers because the toxicity damages their emotional well-being. While others around you may not understand it, this is a decision that you get to make for your own mental health. Cherise reports, "I have learned to have compassion for my mother, knowing about her own hurtful childhood, but today, I choose not to associate with her."

Mandy says, "About six months ago, I made the final attempt to reach my mother emotionally and could not. I feel sorrowful because I do believe in the natural order of relationships, and it would have been nice to have a mother-daughter relationship, but it is not to be and I have accepted that."

"I didn't talk to my mother the last ten years of her life," says Antoinette, 60. "I just couldn't do it anymore. I had spent many years trying to make her love me and trying to make everything okay. It was sad. When she died, I found out from the sheriff. We went to clean things up at her house and found a note on the bulletin board that said that she had forgiven us for being so horrible to her. They sent me her ashes, and I put them in the car. I couldn't even take them into the house. I sold that car and forgot to take the ashes out. It was a little weird calling those people to tell them to destroy the ashes I had left in the old car. People are always shocked that I couldn't make it good with her, but they really don't understand what she was like!"

This sad, extreme example is more common than you might think. I have known daughters who felt tremendous relief when their narcissistic mothers passed away. They feel delivered out from under a huge burden, but guilty about admitting it.

If your mother is indeed unchangeable and you find yourself being constantly abused by her, it is important to know that disconnecting from her can be healthy. When you decide to make this choice, however, make sure that you have completed your own recovery work. If you simply detach and remove yourself from your mother without doing your own work, you will not diminish your pain and your true self cannot emerge to the peacefulness that you desire. As Dr. Murray Bowen reminds us in *Family Therapy in Clinical Practice,* "Less-differentiated people are moved about like pawns by emotional tensions. Better-differentiated people are less vulnerable to tension."[2]

Thankfully, not all mothers with narcissistic traits are lost causes. Daughters do choose to stay in a relationship with more workable mothers, and to create a different kind of connection. I call this "the civil connection."

The Civil Connection

In the civil connection, daughters of narcissistic mothers change the dynamic of their interactions with Mother by having less contact. When they are in touch, they keep the situation light, civil, and polite, but make no attempt to be emotionally close. This is a good option for daughters who do not want to give up their mother totally, but have accepted that she is incapable of true mothering.

The daughter is in touch with her mother without having expectations and consequently suffers few disappointments. This arrangement works best after you have completed your recovery work, which ensures that you have accepted your mother's limitations and separated from her properly. Without having adequately separated, you are at risk for being sucked back into the narcissistic family dynamics. As stated in chapter 11, your goal in separating is to be able to be "a part of and apart from" your mother and family of origin. This means you have developed sound boundaries around yourself. For some daughters who are in the midst of recovery, but not feeling strong enough to be around Mother yet, I recommend a temporary separation.

The Temporary Separation

Although your mother will not typically be happy about this, it can be very helpful for you to take a hiatus from her for a time while you are going through your recovery work. This gives you time to heal and work through the feelings and not be constantly triggered by her behavior. It's perfectly fine to tell Mother that you are grappling with some of your own issues and you need some personal space for a while. You can tell her you will contact her if there is an emergency that she needs to know about and ask that she do the same. She does not have to like this. She may throw a fit. But that's okay—you say it, and then you do it. If she does not leave you alone, you will have to learn to set boundaries with her, which we will discuss below. You are in charge of your life, not your mom. She may up the ante, so to speak, and try some manipulation as the women in the stories below describe, but it is your job to stand your ground. Your recovery is at stake.

- Michaela, 46, says, "I've distanced myself from my mother from time to time, but she finds ways of manipulating me into helping her with things she needs done. This irritates me to no end. If I don't call her back, she calls and calls, like a stalker!"

- And Myra, 38, reports the following with sadness: "About two years ago I became aware of narcissism and realized, after a lifetime of insults, that she is the one with the problem. Since that time, I have been courteous but limited our time together and have definitely set up some separations and long-awaited boundaries. She has been even worse since then; she seems to realize she can't control me anymore. This whole thing makes me sick to my stomach."

You need to know how to set boundaries with your mother, how to make them stick, and how to follow through.

Setting Boundaries with Mother

Setting boundaries means clearly stating what you will do and what you won't do. It is letting people know where you stand and drawing a line they are not allowed to cross. It means setting limits. Many people in general are fearful of setting boundaries because they worry about others' feelings. "If I set a boundary, I will hurt Mother's feelings." Daughters also fear setting a boundary because it will make their mothers angry. "If I told her I was not coming to dinner because I needed to rest and take care of myself, she would be furious!"

A very common reason that daughters don't set good boundaries with their mothers is that they fear abandonment. "If I tell her to back off, she will never speak to me again, and I don't want to lose my mother totally. I've seen her cut off other people and then that's it. She could do this with me too."

Narcissists commonly cut people off and out of their lives due to their shallow emotional style of seeing others as either good or bad. Everything is black or white to them. If you have seen your mother do this, your fear of abandonment is very real. But you must assess it in realistic terms. If she has already abandoned you emotionally, she truly does not have the power to do much more that could wreak equal or similar devastation.

Janelle, 36, cites why she can't set boundaries with her mother. "She will get mad, never forgive me, turn the whole family against me, and then cut me out of the will. I need some inheritance money, and my children deserve that too." This is a decision only you can make, but generally, consider that your own mental health and sanity hold a higher value than money that may or may not be passed on through your mother's will. Learning how to set boundaries for yourself is a way to manage your life, your time, and your health. It is a necessity of healthy living.

So, let's say you have now set a boundary with Mother and told her you will not be seeing her for a while due to your need to focus on some of your own therapeutic issues. You did this by saying to her, "Mom, I am working on some personal issues and I need to tell you that I will not be available for our Sunday dinners for a while. I need some space and will not be calling you. When I am finished, I will let you know. I do not want you to call me during this period, unless it is a bona fide emergency. I am not angry and this is not about you. It is about what I need right now."

Your mother may quite reasonably ask if everything is okay, and you can respond that you are fine and reassure her again that you are not upset with her. If she is indeed narcissistic, she will assume it is about her, so I know you are thinking right now, Oh, no, that won't work! But it will work if you follow through. She may indeed try to manipulate and call and even drop by. Your job is to keep setting the boundary by not responding once you have told her this. She rings the doorbell and you don't answer. She calls you and you don't answer. She stalks you and you tell her again in firm tones that you are serious about this. How she decides to deal with this is her problem and not yours. You are not responsible for her feelings. The key to making boundaries stick is for you to stick to them! You can be very kind about this and gently remind her that you will be back in touch when you are able to do so.

As you begin to get comfortable setting boundaries, you will find it helpful to set boundaries with your mother over many issues and situations. Let's do some practice ones so that you can refer back to them when you are having trouble.

> *Your mother says:* "Honey, there appears to be a lot of dust in your house. Look at the coffee table. I know you're a working mother, but your family deserves a clean, sanitary home."
>
> *You say:* "Mom, this is my house. I am comfortable with my level of housekeeping. I appreciate your concern, but if my family finds this a problem, we will deal with it."

Your mother says: "I brought you some diet pills, honey, because I've noticed you've put on a few pounds lately. I did a lot of research and these are the best I could find."

You say: "Mom, if I decide that my weight is a problem, I will address this issue with my doctor."

Your mother says: "Every time I see my granddaughter, her hair looks like a damn rat's nest. When you were a child, I never let you go out of the house without grooming you properly. Don't you care about how your daughter looks?"

You say: "Mom, I am very proud of my daughter and who she is becoming, and I am not particularly worried about how her hair looks today."

Your mother says: "I need you to call me every day to check on me. I could have a heart attack and you wouldn't even know. I would lie there alone suffering, and what would people think?"

You say: "Mom, if you are really worried about this, there is a practical solution. They make safety alarms that you can wear. This device alerts 911 if there is a medical emergency."

Your mother says: "I can't believe you are actually getting a divorce. What on earth did you do to mess up this marriage, and how am I going to explain this to the family?"

You say: "My relationship decisions are mine to make, and it is very hurtful to me when you cannot be supportive and helpful."

Your mother says: "What do you mean, you're not coming to my house for Thanksgiving? You know how hard I work to cook for this family. You know we always do Thanksgiving at my house. How could you do this to me?"

You say: "Mom, now that I'm married, I want to be involved with my husband's family also. Holidays will be a little bit different from time to time."

Setting firm boundaries allows you to feel comfortable in any situation, particularly when you are with an intrusive mother. It takes practice and restraint, but do not respond to your mother's reaction in a hostile manner. Set the boundary and, if she does not respect it, remove yourself from the situation. You can set healthy boundaries kindly and courteously. You do not have to act angry, resentful, or defensive. You are making a statement and drawing your line in the sand for what you need, how you feel, and sometimes to make a point about what is not okay. Rather than engage in an argument, simply state your boundary over and over until your mother takes your point.

Another strategy for dealing with your mother may be to consider mother-daughter therapy sessions.

Taking Mother to Therapy

When I ask my clients the question "Would your mother attend therapy with you to discuss mother-daughter issues?" most laugh and even scoff a bit. The more narcissistic your mother is, the less likely she will choose to attend therapy with you to address your feelings about your relationship. It is difficult and sometimes impossible for a narcissist to feel her own feelings. She typically projects her emotions onto others and is unable to reach inside to sort and feel. Remember, you can't heal what you cannot feel, so narcissistic mothers usually tend to stay away from their inner emotional life. If your mother has never dealt with feelings or owned her own issues, therapy will be a waste of time. Many mothers walk out of therapy sessions when the issues relate to something that they have done wrong or that is hurtful to the daughters. It is typical of the full-blown narcissist to blame her daughter even in therapy and in front of the therapist.

This puts you in a horrible bind—you yearn for a healthy relationship with your mother and are willing to put the work in, but your mother refuses the notion that she needs help.

- Rosanne, 30, tells me, "I couldn't get my mom to go to therapy with me. But while I was in therapy, I talked to her about it. She was a freakin' basket case! She denied everything. All I wanted to hear was 'I'm sorry' and all she could do was cry and say she had such a horrible daughter. Crying. Victim. No empathy. I would never ask her to go to therapy again."

- Monica's mother tried going to therapy with her, but ended up fighting the process and blaming Monica, while also worrying about her image as a mother. "Going to therapy with Mom was a trip! She would go, but it was a disaster. She got very defensive and it really was an exercise in her not hearing a word I was saying because she was too concerned about herself and how she looked to the therapist."

In many situations, mothers who have fewer narcissistic traits are actually open to learning and growing. With these mothers, there is hope that healing can happen between mother and daughter both in therapy and outside of therapy. Most daughters know instinctively if their mother is a candidate for this or not. They can tell based on their prior experiences with Mom when they attempted to discuss feelings or difficulties in communicating. Even though it is hard for mothers to deal with, some can look at themselves clearly and decide they want to work on the important relationship with their daughter or daughters.

My client Gerda, 62, admitted to having some narcissistic traits and was also a daughter of a mother with severe NPD. She had had significant pain in her own relationship with her late mother, whose emotional hold was as strong as it had ever been. Gerda could see the negative effects on her life and how these had affected her own parenting. She truly wanted to work on healing with her three daughters. Unfortunately, the daughters were too hurt and saddened to try. They had given up on Gerda and did not believe in her ability to change, so the mother-daughter sessions have yet to take place. Being ever hopeful, I think there will be a day when I can see them all together. Sometimes daughters have to do their own recovery work first in order to be ready to face Mom and all that therapy entails. The daughters are young and still have some work to do, but are lovely people about whom I feel very hopeful in the long run.

Time is a big factor to consider when determining if you will do therapy with your mother or not. Sometimes the timing is not right and it is more productive to wait until all parties are ready. The mother, Gerda, was able to step back, do her own recovery and address the generational issues with her daughters. I rarely see this, and I continue to tell her she is amazing and I am so proud of her.

If you do begin mother-daughter therapy and your mother is abusive or emotionally shut off and blames you for everything, I suggest that you stop the session and talk alone with the therapist. Ask whether or not it seems productive to continue having your mother in session with you. The therapist should be your ally in this recovery process and helpful to you. Your sessions should not perpetuate the abuse and blame that your mother has already heaped on you. If you feel strongly that you do not want to continue with your mother and your therapist disagrees, you will need to take some time to think about your decision carefully. In the end, trust your own intuition about whether or not the time is right.

What to Tell Mother About Your Own Therapy

This book gives the steps in the recovery program that I use with my clients so that you can do your own personal therapeutic work. That said, working with a therapist one on one can be extremely beneficial for you during this time as well. If you decide to go this route, please keep in mind that it is up to you and you alone whether or not to tell your mother that you are even attending therapy. Therapy is a confidential relationship for a reason, and no one needs to know you attend unless you want to tell them. This includes your mother.

If you decide to tell her, you should also decide how much you want to share with her. You may choose to inform her that you are attending, but tell her that you do not plan to share this private experience with her. If she pushes for information, gently set up your boundaries. If these do not work, set even firmer boundaries. An example of each is below.

A gentle boundary: "Mother, I appreciate your interest in my therapy, and when I am ready to discuss it with you, I will likely do that. I am still in the midst of some confusion and trying to understand myself better and want to get further along before I can discuss it clearly and appropriately with you. Thank you for understanding that."

A firm boundary: "Mother, I need to be very clear with you that my therapy is confidential and I do not discuss it with anyone. It is designed to help me with some issues I am experiencing in *my* life right now. Do not ask me about it, as I do not plan to share that information with you."

You can preface these boundaries with "I care about you and your feelings," or "I love you, Mom, but . . ." If Mother acts hurt or gets angry, it is her job to take care of her own feelings, not your job to fix them. Detach from the scene and let it be her problem—which it is. Remember, setting boundaries is not a mean thing to do; it is a healthy exercise in taking good care of yourself. Typically, we daughters know this, but because Mother is good at making us feel guilty, it is sometimes difficult to do. Remind yourself that you do not create feelings in other people. Each person is responsible for his or her own feelings and reactions and therefore must also be accountable for them.

The Real Work Is Within

As I am sure you are finding out, dealing with your mother is much easier after working on your own recovery. The reasons for this change are many: You are less reactive to her projections; you can set clear boundaries; because of your grief work, she is less able to trigger your pain; and because you have accepted that she has limitations, you no longer have great expectations of her. Regardless of whether or not you are practicing a complete separation, a temporary separation, or the civil connection, your success is determined by your own internal healing.

What If Mother Is Deceased?

If your mother has passed away, you will not be engaging in some of the exercises above. Nonetheless, your internal healing is still a must. I have treated many daughters who continue to have legacy issues throughout their lives even after their mother has died. The nasty messages stay stuck until you consciously loosen and release them from within you. Working on your recovery is necessary for you to be healthy.

Let's explore a deeper understanding of your mother and her background.

Understanding Mother's Makeup

Because most daughters are codependent, it is a bit tricky to ask daughters of narcissistic mothers to take some time to understand their mother's background, origins, and how she became who she is. By doing this, you won't let her off the hook, minimize your own pain, or make your wounds suddenly invisible again. You will not be making it "all about Mom" again. But this exercise can help settle your insides and give you a grasp of the larger picture. To use an analogy, let's imagine that I am going to hike or climb to the summit of a very high mountain with complex topography. I know that I will have to start at the bottom and work my way up and I imagine that I will have many obstacles to overcome as I go. If I could fly over this mountain in a helicopter first or look at a good map to see what I am up against in the big picture, it would prepare me better for the climb. The map or overview would not diminish the difficulty of my journey or my efforts; it would simply assist in my overall planning and ultimate success. The same is true if you better understand where your mother comes from. This work is to help *you*.

So to start with, try to find out if your mother had a narcissistic parent—mother or father. It is very likely that she did. You can take some of the characteristics we have defined in this book and ask her those very questions about her parents. Many narcissistic mothers are quite willing to talk about their backgrounds if it does not involve something that they did. My parents, for example, were able to give several vivid examples of their parents' behaviors. We had a very animated, pleasant, but admittedly short discussion; nonetheless, it was better than none. I was able to trace some of the family legacy from this and use it to explain some of my own experience with my grandparents.

Next, you can ask relatives. Aunts, uncles, and cousins are great resources. Living grandparents who are not narcissistic are another great resource. Sometimes, after a narcissistic spouse passes, a relative is more willing to share thoughts and memories.

Of course, these discussions cannot take place in many families. If your family would not countenance it, you know it. Just let it go. Do not cause yourself unneeded drama if you are sure it won't be successful. Trust your own intuition. I know of some daughters who pushed the issue with relatives and, when it did not work out well, blamed themselves for it. I do not want that to happen for you.

Other resources include close friends of the family who knew your parents and grandparents well. Although rare these days, some families still live in the same towns and cities where the whole extended family grew up.

If you cannot get specifics about narcissism, you can ask your mother general questions about her upbringing. Questions such as:

- Did you have a happy childhood?
- Did you feel loved by your parents?
- Did you feel you got enough attention growing up?
- Did your parents talk to you about feelings?
- Were you listened to and did you feel heard?
- How were you disciplined when your parents were upset with you?
- Were you encouraged as an individual or did you have to fit the mold for the family image of what was expected?
- Was your mother or father particularly concerned about what others thought?

The more you can learn about your mother's background, the better you will understand her and why she acts the way she does. She most likely was an unmothered child herself who has her own significant trauma in her background.

When attempting to retrieve further information, however, you may feel as if you're digging in the dark. Be prepared for her to have a lot of denial about her own childhood. While your mother will likely not be the best reporter of information, see what she is willing to share. Accept whatever that is.

Also look at your mother's parenting as influenced by her generation and time. A multitude of factors influence how every mother parents.

Historical Perspectives

We are all shaped significantly by societal values and expectations of parenting. Each generation seems to have its own set of parenting philosophies and beliefs with which to contend, so one generation may contradict the next. See the birth markers as defined by *Genera-*

tions: Working Together, below.[3] As examples, I have listed the women in my legacy. You can do the same to gain some perspective of the big picture of your own family.

GENERATION	BIRTH YEARS	EXAMPLE
The GI Generation	1901–1923	My Grandmother
The Silent Generation	1924–1945	My Mother
The Baby Boom Generation	1946–1964	Me
Generation X	1965–1980	My Daughter
The Millennial Generation		
(sometimes called Gen Y)	1981–2002	My Granddaughters

Parenting beliefs across the ages have gone from "spare the rod and spoil the child" and "children should be seen and not heard" to the attitude of baby boomers who try to build their children's self-esteem without requiring them to become competent in academic and social skills. That's a seismic shift right there. Many would say, "How in the world does anyone raise a child in the right way?"

Baby boomer mothers moved from the Donna Reed model of the stay-at-home, baking cookies, be-there-at-all-times mother, to highly educated mothers who had careers outside the home. The prevailing concept of womanhood at the time I had my first child, for example, was undergoing a cultural revolution. Mothers became feminists, joined demonstrations for equal rights, and began careers. Family structure changed: Divorce, latchkey kids, single-parent homes, and day-care centers became common, where they had been unfamiliar to the previous generation. My own daughter, in a fit of anger one day, called me a "house-divorcée," somehow getting the unspoken message that it was no longer appropriate to call her mother a "house-wife."

Baby boomer mothers paved the way for their daughters to have better education and health care, and equal access to schools and careers. They created choices that women did not previously have. Yet some of their Gen X daughters believe that, while their mothers were doing this, the family suffered and the daughters felt secondary to their mothers' career aspirations. This controversy requires sensitive communication between mothers and daughters, but the mothers' commitment to self-development and career success is *not* the same as narcissism, unless the mothers display narcissistic traits. At the same time, baby boomer mothers need to acknowledge their Gen X daughters' feelings and understand that they can relate to some of the daughters in this book. Understanding, empathy, and communication are the keys for resolution.

In any case, given the effects of their culture, society, and history on our mothers and grandmothers, it is not surprising that they didn't know how best to be parents much of the time. It is safe to say that many parented in the way that they were parented. Having some understanding of the historical perspective makes it a bit easier to understand how maternal attitudes and behavior can change from one generation to the next and vulnerable girls grow up to become narcissistic mothers.

That said, however, I am not offering an excuse, but only fodder for further understanding. I do believe that for any generation the trademark of good mothering is the ability to give authentic love and empathy, and physical and emotional care, no matter the historical moment.

With this understanding of our mothers' histories, let's look now at the complicated concept of forgiveness.

Forgiveness

The word "forgiveness" is laden with meaning and misunderstanding. Many daughters were taught at a very early age that nice girls forgive and forget. The clear message is that we are expected to forgive anyone who has hurt us because it is the right thing to do.

While I do believe in the rightness and importance of forgiveness and in the emotional benefits it can give you, I do see it in a different light. Forgiveness is positive and healing when we can see that the person's intentions were not to hurt us. But we do ourselves no good when we try to deny the pain we felt. And we can actually set ourselves up for further harm when we don't deal with the reality that we were hurt and that the person is likely to hurt us again—whether inadvertently or on purpose.

Many people misconstrue forgiveness as somehow condoning the original offending behavior, as if saying that it is all right. But I believe that accountability is crucial for mental health. So I counsel you to pardon only someone who is accountable for her behavior, when she has owned up to it, has become conscious of it, and is truly sorry for having done it. While this may sound harsh, not many narcissistic mothers do this, so I do not advocate pardons for most of them.

I do advise that you practice a kind of inner letting go, however—for your own good. Daughters of narcissistic mothers have been unloved, and many have been abused physically, sexually, and emotionally. We do not condone bad mothering. We do not condone ignoring the basic needs and rights of children. But you do have to let go of this past internally, so that you, the daughter, can also let go of your anger, rage, and sadness. You forgive by forgoing these negative emotions so that you can go on for the rest of your life.

Step One of the grief process allows you to accomplish the internal letting go. Afterward, you will have an internal feeling that is more neutral; you will no longer have the intense emotions you once associated with your mother. This neutrality allows you to keep that feeling of letting go. It feels like internal forgiveness. It is your gift to yourself. As my client Kenna shares:

- "Although I could never talk about emotions with my mother—she has the emotions of a doorknob—I am now able to say I love her. The funny thing is she didn't even notice that I didn't say this before. I now get that this recovery and forgiveness deal is for me. It feels so good."

This kind of forgiveness is an understanding of your mother that allows you to grow past your old feelings of being a saddened, hurt child. This kind of forgiveness feels adult-like. Lewis Smedes, in *Shame and Grace: Healing the Shame We Don't Deserve,* puts it like this:

> The first and often the only person to be healed by forgiveness is the person who does the forgiveness. . . . When we genuinely forgive, we set a prisoner free and then discover that the prisoner we set free was us.[4]

My theory and practice of forgiveness is not the only way. Many daughters find it helpful to draw on their religious or spiritual backgrounds to help them forgive. Twelve-step addiction programs advocate that true forgiveness is when you can wish the person well who has hurt you and pray for her to have all that she wishes for. They also take it a step further and suggest that you pray for the hurtful person to have all the things that you want for yourself—health, wealth, and happiness. Henry Nouwen writes in *The Only Necessary Thing*:

> Forgiveness is the name of love practiced among people who love poorly. The hard truth is that all of us love poorly. We need to forgive and be forgiven every day, every hour, unceasingly. That is the great work of love among the fellowship of the weak that is the human family.[5]

My main concern for your recovery is that the form of forgiveness that you choose to implement eradicates blame so thoroughly that you have no traces of feeling like a victim. For if you continue to live in a victim mentality, you are at risk of defining your life based on your wounds. That would mean that you were allowing yourself to be controlled by your mother's failures. Being free from the feeling of victimization is a true sign of recovery.

Mother's Gifts

It is important to remember that no person is all good or all bad. Whether your mother has narcissistic traits or has a full-blown NPD, she has some goodness in her. She likely passed along talents, passions, interests, and knowledge to you. Remind yourself of the gifts she has given you. They might be artistic, musical, mechanical, body shape or size, texture of hair, beautiful eyes, smooth skin, or something like the ability to paper a wall without a single wrinkle.

Write in your journal about the gifts your mother has bestowed upon you and allow yourself to feel gratitude. When I was a small child, my grandmother used a significant, repetitive phrase with me. If I ever attempted to say anything bad about anyone, she would sit me on her lap and gently tell me, "If you look hard enough, you can always find the gold in people." I have certainly found this to be true. Look for the gold and those gifts in your mother. It will help you more than you may realize right now. Suzie read this to me from her journal:

> From our home I left with a feisty spirit. Perhaps not equipped for most practical things in life, I did learn that honesty and integrity were my greatest assets. I learned a work ethic that is highly valued. I learned that high standards yield high results in most things. I learned humor and laughter would bridge most differences for short-term gains. I learned table manners, how to set a table and entertain. I learned social skills. I learned to shop! Somehow I emerged tenacious; I look for the best in others, forgive easily, and learn quickly. I painfully learned I wanted to be a different kind of mother, so I was motivated to teach myself about nurturing parenting. As a result, the greatest joy in my life has been being a mom. The cycle is broken.

Love, Not Blame: The Look of Recovery

My hope for you includes all of the following: You now view yourself with an inner knowing and a sense of love. You replaced the anxiety and unease of your childhood with a flood of gratitude for having been given life *and* this important journey to undertake. You now understand that the path you were given to travel was and is full of life lessons worth treasuring. You have recognized that you have an inner wisdom that you can now share with your children, others whom you love, and the world. You now see that your mother gave you special gifts, although they were disguised and hidden in trauma, that you can now appreciate.

You are accountable for your own life. You depend on yourself to manage your emotions. You are an adult with a solid sense of self. You take yourself seriously and are no longer filled with self-doubt. You have stepped out of the shadows of a childhood filled with anxiety into the sunshine of confidence and competence.

Now you are ready to complete the healing journey by undertaking the final step to ending the legacy of your narcissistic mother.

CHAPTER FOURTEEN

FILLING THE EMPTY MIRROR

ENDING THE NARCISSISTIC LEGACY

Traumata stored in the brain but denied by our conscious
minds will always be visited on the next generation.
—Alice Miller, online interview[1]

In this chapter, you'll learn how to use your awareness of the narcissistic legacy and your desire to change it, to stop it from being passed along to your own children. Daughters of narcissistic mothers commonly express fears that they may have learned or acquired narcissistic traits that then adversely affect their most intimate relationships in the roles of mothers, lovers, and friends. Elan Golomb, in *Trapped in the Mirror*, expresses this worrisome thought: "If the parent has a narcissistic bent, the pressure to copy is strong."[2]

A Look at Parenting

For readers who have children, this topic is of great importance. Many women I've interviewed express fears about their own parenting. Young mothers are typically more optimistic about their parenting skills, but as they and their children get older, some women begin to see some familiar effects of narcissistic behavior in their children. Understandably they begin to panic.

- "I tried to do everything different from my mother in raising my own children, and we still had problems. What can I do now that they are becoming teens and young adults?" pleads Scarlett, who is now in her fifties. "I see my children not being accountable for their behavior and using substance abuse as a way to numb feelings. This terrifies me."

Here's what I believe happened in my own pass down to my children (admittedly, this is only my perception and my children may disagree). As I was growing up, I had pinpointed many things that I did *not* want to do as a parent, and as an adult, I spent years studying child development and psychology to support me in changing generational patterns. From the moment my first child was born, I worked earnestly to parent differently. Despite all of this, I learned the hard way that how we behave in general *shouts* at our children, while our direct parenting interactions with them seem more like whispers. Even though I did everything I could to be as good a parent as possible, I still ended up modeling for them that I did not feel good enough within myself. This went on for a long period of time, until I entered my intensive recovery program. Of course, I never told my children that they were not good enough (nor did I ever believe that for a minute), but they saw in my own struggle for worthiness how I viewed myself. It feels as if I inadvertently modeled that nasty message and so passed it on against my will. In my clinical research, I have seen the same with other daughters.

The behaviors and attitudes that we model for our children are of the utmost importance. Because we can unconsciously pass along negative beliefs and attitudes, our own recovery as mothers is a *must*. I am dedicated to educating other women about this risk and necessity so that we can all work to eradicate the painful legacy of narcissism from our lives and our children's lives.

I am sure I have many other blind spots as a parent. My commitment to myself and my children is to keep all doors open for healing.

I encourage you to do the same. To open the passageway for new understanding of each other is a great gift, one that for most adult daughters could never become more than a dream because our own mothers could not be open to change. The good news is that it is entirely possible to change for our children and to change their legacy.

Begin to assess your own parenting. Acknowledge the painful reality that it is impossible to be a child of a narcissist and not be *somewhat* impaired narcissistically. Anyone raised this way has probably acquired a few traits of narcissism. I know this is not what you want to hear—I had trouble admitting it to myself—but you must face this before you can attempt to remedy it.

Remember that narcissism is a spectrum disorder. Full-blown narcissistic personality disorder sits at the extreme negative end of the continuum, but most people exist around the other end. Most people have some self-regard, and this is normal.

When you begin to work on accountability in this area, you may find that no one around you is as supportive or reassuring as you would like. Your own inner voice may chime in and tell you this is yet another sign of "not being good enough." I want to be clear and supportive with you on this matter: Identifying your own narcissistic traits and working on them *is* responsible and self-nurturing, and it proves that you are taking yourself and your recovery seriously. The greatest gift you can give yourself is to learn to manage and control your own feelings and behavior. Remember, your recovery is lifelong. You can't tie it to one minute or the next. There is no need to feel shame or guilt. You are taking yourself out of the "victim" role and developing an adult self that is strong, self-reliant, and loving—a self that is quite *good enough*.

You do not travel alone in your desire to be a good-enough parent. Few things in life carry the responsibility and weight of being a mother. The same awareness and desire also carry forward into being a grandmother and a great-grandmother. Your maternal instinct to do it right is a deep longing of the female soul. We all make mistakes and wish we could do better. When we make mistakes with our kids, it is difficult to let ourselves off the hook, because the errors affect those we love the most. Even if you had no narcissism in your background, it would still be impossible to be a perfect parent. I have yet to meet one. In fact, if someone ever came to me in my role of mental health provider and claimed to be perfect in the parenting realm, I would likely grab the *DSM* and begin to assess some kind of delusional disorder. I will always remember the day that my best friend, Kay, said to me after discussing some parental mistakes we both made, "I sure do like you better, Karyl, now that you have taken yourself out of the race for mother of the year!"

Below are key tools to parenting in a healthy manner—without narcissism.

Empathy

Empathy tops my list, as it is the cornerstone for love. Lack of empathy is, of course, a trademark of narcissistic mothers. Empathizing with your children is feeling what they are feeling and acknowledging those feelings. It is the art of compassion and sensitivity, as well as the ability to give moral support in whatever they are experiencing. You do not have to agree with them, but you are there for them. You put aside your own feelings and thoughts for the moment and tune in to their emotional needs to attempt to understand where they are coming from and why. Instead of citing rules or trying to give advice and direction, try this empathy exercise instead.

To empathize involves identifying the feelings your child is expressing and telling him or her that you recognize the feeling in the moment: "I hear that you are angry." "You are feeling sad." "I see that you are very upset." Being able to show empathy to a child at any age makes him or her feel real as well as important as a person.

This is difficult to do when a child is upset with you. Whenever you find your child's feelings to be threatening or upsetting, remember that empathizing is not agreeing, it is acknowledging a real feeling. For example, my five-year-old granddaughter asked for a cookie before dinner. I said, "No, we can have one after dinner." In a typical five-year-old manner, she then said, "I hate you, Nana." Well, I know she doesn't hate me and so does she, but she was angry that she did not get a cookie right then, and that was okay. I was able to say to her, "Honey, I know you don't hate your Nana, but you are mad right now because you want that cookie, and I understand that. I would like to have a cookie, too, right now, but we have to wait until after dinner. It is okay to talk about our mad feelings, though, and I am glad you told me." In this example, my granddaughter needed to feel validated and acknowledged—then she was just fine. The temptation in situations like this is to get angry back at the child and even punish her, which only makes the child feel as if she has to stuff or muffle her own feelings. Your anger or punishment will also make the situation worse, and feelings will escalate.

Older children and teens often are purposely disrespectful to you. In this situation, you do have to set boundaries, but in order for your child to feel heard, you still have to acknowledge the feelings behind the words. For example, an out-of-control teen may call her mother a derogatory name because she is angry about not being able to go to the mall, but the mother must set limits and consequences for this abusive behavior. At the same time, she can acknowledge the feeling that the child is upset. It is surprising to parents, the first time they do this, how effective it is in deflating kids' balloons of anger. The child can often become more reasonable because she has been seen and heard. She has been given a voice.

When my son was about 12 years old, he came home from school one day very angry and began throwing things around in a huff. When we later sat down to dinner, he picked up a plate and slammed it on the table. My first instinct was to tell him to knock it off and go to his room, but I said, "Honey, something is terribly wrong. You are very angry. Let's talk about what is wrong." This immediately deflated the big red balloon of anger and he was able to express his feelings of being upset with his sister for something I can't really remember. I know now, and knew then, that if I had sent him to his room or immediately punished him, his behavior would have escalated and we probably would never have gotten to the true feelings. Whatever he was angry about was much less important than acknowledging his feelings at the moment. He got to have a voice and be heard, and I was rewarded by no broken dishes!

Accountability

Being accountable for your own feelings and behavior is vital to your mental health and peace of mind. As daughters of narcissistic mothers, what we saw most of the time was the "blame game" in action. Mother was typically not accountable for her behavior or feelings and projected them constantly onto others—and particularly onto us.

When you are practicing accountability, you adopt a viewpoint that says, No matter what happens to me, it is my responsibility to manage my own feelings and behavior. No one can create my feelings, cause me to drink, force me to be aggressive toward others, make me depressed, make me hit or yell at my children, or drive too fast, or not follow the law, etc. I make my own decisions and have choices about almost everything. I am only a victim if I choose to be one.

It is also important to teach your children that they need to be accountable for their behavior. You do that by setting boundaries and limits for them and imposing safe, healthy consequences on them whenever they overstep these limits. You do not use harsh disciplinary techniques or anything that smacks of shame or humiliation. You provide and consistently enforce boundaries about right and wrong with consequences that are age-appropriate.

If children are not taught accountability for their actions, they grow up with a feeling of entitlement, which is a trait of narcissism.

Entitlement

While it is important for our children to feel special in our eyes, it is not important for them to feel special in everyone's eyes. It is imperative that they truly believe other people's needs are just as important as theirs. You can teach your children that by modeling respect for others, and by teaching them to appreciate that each individual has his own special qualities to bring to the world. A child can learn to see herself as unique, but also as one of many people in a large community of human beings on earth. She does not have to stand out from the crowd to be fulfilled or have peace within. To ensure that you are not encouraging entitlement in your children, focus on guiding, directing, and assisting them in gathering a sense of consciousness about their place in the world around them and their connections and responsibilities to others.

Many parents seem to be pressuring their kids in academics and sports to be the best at all costs. This pressure to "have" and to "achieve" too often bypasses basic principles of personal accountability. Do not overrate your child's abilities or talents. Be realistic about her accomplishments and give her credit for what she does achieve. Be involved in her successes and praise her for what she accomplishes, but don't push her to the point that she feels "not good enough" for not living up to your expectations. This can create confusion, resentment, and a sense of entitlement in your child.

Values

Teaching children values is crucial to their development, but of course you first have to know what you believe in and what you don't. In talking to hundreds of people in psychotherapy sessions over the years, I am constantly amazed at how many folks don't know what to say when I ask them about their worldview or their value system. Since you've gone through your own recovery, however, you now have an understanding of your beliefs and values. I hope that you see how crucial it is to teach the importance of honesty, integrity, kindness, empathy and compassion for others, forgiveness, healthy self-esteem and self-care, and the difference between what is right and wrong. These days, many parents seem to pay more attention to how their child looks than to how he or she treats others.

The best way to teach a value system is to model it for your children. Show them that values matter by dealing with them and others honestly, kindly, compassionately, and with integrity. Teach them the importance of self-respect and self-care by taking good care of yourself. Use examples from the neighborhood, television, movies, school, and the daily news to discuss your values. Whatever activity your child is involved in can become a classroom for teaching a value and modeling right from wrong. Be careful not to be harsh, critical, or judgmental. Simply express and show how you would handle a situation kindly, assertively, and with integrity.

Make sure that your children's activities involve giving to others or helping in some way. At first, they may just learn to be helpful to others, and eventually they can perform work in the community. Giving back teaches that other people are important.

Value Their Personhood,
Not Only Their Accomplishments

Your love for your children needs to be based on who they are and not merely what they can do. As the daughter of a narcissistic mother, you were taught that what you did was more important than who you were, so you likely grew up feeling that your parents did not even know the real you.

Know who your children are. Know what they like and dislike and what they are interested in separate from you and your interests. Value their good-heartedness and kindness as well as their sense of humor and intelligence. Don't define them by what they do (my son the soccer player, my daughter the ballet dancer). If you allow your children's self-esteem to be centered on their accomplishments, you are setting up another generation of achievement-dependent narcissists who have to be "stars" to feel good about themselves. Give them credit where credit is due whenever they realize their goals or visions. Let them know that you are very proud of what they have done and that you will also love them just as much if they do not become CEOs or star basketball players.

When I was working on this book, an old friend called me to catch up. He told me that his son had just received a baseball scholarship for college, but talked more about his son's "big heart" than about his scholarship! My friend is proud of his son's accomplishment, but also really loves his son for who he is. What an artful balance.

Authenticity

Encourage your child to be real. Authentic expression of self and feelings is the route to becoming a centered person. We daughters learned to be fake in the narcissistic system. Don't pass the image focus on to your kids. They can be appropriate and real as well as assertive and respectful of others and their boundaries. It is okay to be who you are even if some people prefer something else. Not everyone has to like you or your children.

Allowing authenticity means accepting your child's feelings and encouraging her to express them even if you disagree or they upset you. It means that you don't teach her to lie to look good, or to deny what she perceives as real. No more elephants in the living room that no one discusses but everyone knows are there; don't have dysfunctional secrets in the family and ask your child to keep them to himself. You can teach him that he does not have to lie to himself or others to keep up an image. We all know from painful experience how crazy-making that is.

I recently observed a mother tell her crying child, "We don't cry.

People don't like sad children." The child quickly clammed up. It was obvious that this was a familiar message to her. The danger in doing this with children is that it teaches them to deny their feelings, sacrifice their true selves, and adopt an "image" that is acceptable to the parent. Guard against this in your communications with your children. If you pressure them to put on a facade, you leave them no choice but to believe that their true selves are unacceptable.

Parental Hierarchy

Your children are not supposed to be your friends. Keep boundaries between parents and children. All children are meant to be on the same level. Don't share adult information with them and overload them with your adult problems. Refer to the healthy family hierarchy in chapter 4: It is not your children's job to meet your needs. It is your job to meet theirs.

Maintain appropriate boundaries for each person's separate space in the family and in the home. Respect each other's property and personal bodily space. Teach children how to say no in assertive ways so that they are not walked over by others. This will help them develop a separate sense of self.

Parenting a child is a monumental task, the most rewarding and the most difficult you may undertake. No one can do it perfectly. That's just fine. If you are aware of the above factors, however, you allow yourself a healthier awareness than your parents had when raising you. That in itself is a tremendous gift.

Relationships with Others

Narcissistic traits that you unwittingly acquired will also haunt you in your relationships with other adults. Recognize these traits so that you can get control of them. This will be difficult, but that does not mean you are not a good person. Nor does it mean that you are not good enough. It means that you are human, and you have issues related to a painful, difficult childhood. As an adult, however, you want to become totally accountable, to take an honest look in the mirror. You can move past the pain and sadness and experience, and allow yourself to grow emotionally, and integrate the many complex parts of yourself.

The Internal Mother as Your Guide

You can readily recognize your growth, or lack thereof, in love relationships because they trigger our innermost unmet needs. In love, we attempt to overcome past traumas, but usually we are looking to our love partners to give us the love lacked in childhood. These attempts are misguided, but we repeat them until we complete recovery. This is why so many daughters of narcissistic mothers go through many failed relationships.

Rely on your own internal mother. Learn to re-parent and freshly parent the wounded child by allowing yourself to feel the self-respect that your internal mother provides. Clean out the trauma so that positive new messages stay within you and so that you can rely on the internal mother. Then you can adjust your "relationship picker" so that you are attracted to different kinds of appropriate lovers who are not dependent or codependent. If you need to work further on the internal mother, refer back to chapter 12.

Finding the Love of Your Life

It is time now to throw away the old criteria for how you were choosing and behaving with love partners. If you are accustomed to listing image characteristics such as, "Is he good looking?" "Is he financially well off?" "Does he have an impressive job?" "Does he drive a classy car?" "Can he dance?" now is the time to start asking different questions. "Is he good-looking on the inside?" "Can he manage his own feelings and behavior like he manages his own company?" "Can he show and feel authentic feelings and display empathy?" "Can he genuinely love himself and me?" "Can he dance internally with his own soul and mine?" Now that you are well along the recovery trail, consider choosing a lifetime mate according to the following meaningful factors. If you are in a marriage or relationship, consider whether these factors are present enough.

(The reference to "he," below, is for convenience only and does not imply that the information is intended only for heterosexual relationships.)

- When you are with him, is he kind and compassionate? Does he act with integrity?
- Is he committed to, and does he have the capacity for, a lifetime of learning and growing with you?
- Is he capable of genuine empathy? Is he interested in working through pain and problems?
- Does he have his own personal style, life, interests, hobbies, and passions—separate from yours?
- Are most of your values and worldviews (philosophies of life) similar?
- Do you share common interests so that you can be playful and spend leisure time together that you both enjoy?
- Does he have a sense of humor? Does he use it without hostility but with a good heart?
- Does he want to be your best friend and soul mate, and is he capable of being that? (Does he act like your best friend?)
- Does he talk about his feelings and yours, and is he in touch with his own emotional world?)
- Can he handle ambivalence and shades of gray and not be too rigid about failures and weaknesses in you, himself, and others?
- Does he add to your soul life as well as your material life, thereby making your world a wonderful place to be when you are in it together?
- Does he bring out the best in you?

Your Recovery Tasks in Love Relationships

Now that you are choosing a different kind of love relationship or working to enhance your current one, what do you have to be aware of in your own recovery? You can find the mate that matches the authentic love list, but unless you keep on the path to recovery, your relationship will be unhappy and unsatisfying. Here are your important tasks for relationship work:

- Remember to reciprocate. The relationship has to be a give-and-take, and you need to be able to give and receive with grace and love.
- Your love for him is for the person that he is, not what he can do for you or what you can do for him.
- If or when your unfinished business with Mother gets triggered, go back to the healing steps and work on them, fully owning that this is your work to do. If he is interested in working on it with you, he is a "prince" for sure, but it is primarily your job.
- Let him know in the very beginning that your trust was impaired in early childhood and that trust is a lifelong recovery issue for you. Continue to work on trust issues without projecting them onto him.
- Fight your own dependency needs so that you do not behave in dependent or codependent ways with him. Interdependency is a must for a healthy relationship.
- Keep boundaries around your personal space and encourage him to do the same as well. Allow each other privacy when needed. Whenever this is difficult, discuss it promptly.
- Be authentic and yourself at all times.
- Take care of yourself physically, emotionally, spiritually, and intellectually. Expect him to do this as well, but know that you cannot control or demand it.

- Above all, be accountable for your own feelings and behavior.
- If he is ever misguided and tells you that you are acting "just like your mother," gently tell him never to say that again.

You and Your Friends

Choosing and keeping cherished friends can be a challenge for daughters of narcissistic mothers, but many of the keys in healthy relationships discussed above can apply to friends, too, especially reciprocity, dependency, codependency, and boundaries.

Reciprocity is essential to a healthy friendship. There has to be a give-and-take just like in love relationships. This give-and-take does not have to always be at the same moment, but in general there should be a balance. If one friend is always the giver and one friend is always the taker, the relationship is either dependent or codependent. If you happen to be going through a time when you know you cannot be reciprocal due to some life crisis or big project in which you are involved, let your friends know this. Don't be unfair to yourself and to them and give anyway if you are being drained by your own crisis—inform them and reassure them that you will be back to reciprocating when your crisis is over. The high-achieving daughters have the most difficulty with this, because they are used to being very busy and sometimes do not know how to handle this. They give up friendships because they feel too guilty at not being able to give all the time. This is not necessary with good friends.

Setting boundaries when hurtful things are said to you is important as well. To maintain an authentic friendship, you have to be able to respond to an offensive statement or action with, "That was hurtful to me." Or, "I would be more comfortable if you did not talk about this or do this right now." If your friend is alarmed or amazed, then you need to explain yourself and talk it through. Setting clear boundaries and discussing those boundaries are part of being authentic with the people we care about.

Many daughters of narcissistic mothers report that they have difficulty with female friendships. The reason most cited is that women friends are more emotionally draining and have too many unrealistic expectations of the friendship. I believe that this reaction to female friends is a carryover from the narcissistic mother who was entitled, needy, and demanding so much of the time. If a female friend begins to act like this, you may recoil and run for cover before exploring what is really going on. You may not be communicating well enough for the friend to understand your own needs and boundaries, or you may be choosing friends who are similar to your mother. In the latter case, you may need to start exploring new friendships with women who are emotionally strong and whose interests are similar to yours. Find women friends who can add to your life, rather than drain you. Search for female friendships that offer a match to your strength and celebrate your authenticity and passions in life. Too often daughters complain that other women are competitive and jealous, which may be a flashback to their childhood. Make sure that those friendships are not simply triggering an internal collapse before you write them off. But if the women are competitive and jealous—narcissistic—avoid them if possible. Find authentic female friends who celebrate you and allow you to celebrate them. Such women are a celestial gift and very much worth expending the effort to find. Spending time around healthy people is a must.

The Mirror

Chances are you have been assessing yourself as you have read through this book and you may have found some narcissistic traits on which you need to work. Facing them honestly is very important for your recovery to be complete. You don't have to feel bad about them or "not good enough"—you just need to be accountable. Below is a version of the nine narcissistic traits listed in the *DSM* (*Diagnostic and*

Statistical Manual of Mental Disorders)—the same traits you reviewed in regard to your mother. Let's look at the checklist:

AM I NARCISSISTICALLY IMPAIRED?

1. Do I exaggerate my accomplishments and say I have done things I have not done? Do I act more important than others?
2. Am I unrealistic about my thoughts and desires regarding love, beauty, success, intelligence? Do I seek power in these things?
3. Do I believe that I am so special and unique that only the best institutions and the highest academic professionals could possibly understand me?
4. Do I need to be admired all the time to the point of excess?
5. Do I have a sense of entitlement and expect to be treated differently and with more status than others?
6. Do I exploit others to get what I want or need?
7. Do I lack empathy and therefore never see what others are feeling or needing? Can I put myself in other people's shoes? Can I show empathy?
8. Am I jealous and competitive with others or unreasonably, without logic, think that others are jealous of me?
9. Am I a haughty person who acts arrogant and "better than" with my friends, colleagues, and family?

And I would add one more:
10. Am I capable of authentic love?[3]

Very few daughters of narcissistic mothers would answer all of these questions in the affirmative, but you may see some areas that fit you. Use this list as a measuring stick for your personal growth. The two most important attributes for a healthy self and for motherhood are the ability to love and show empathy. Most daughters do possess an innate maternal instinct even though they may feel the need to polish it.

• • •

You are on your way to recovery. You have faced your past and your-self honestly and with a sense of urgency. By now you have experienced old pain and the dawn of a new freedom from your past as well as the freedom to become yourself. You know that you cannot heal the things you cannot feel, and you have opened yourself to a new, fearless way of thinking and living your life. You know how to express yourself and your needs directly and clearly. You have freed yourself from unrealistic expectations and can follow your own values and passions. My heart will always be with you as you continue on your lifelong path of recovery and discovery.

NOTES

CHAPTER 1

1. Elan Golomb, Ph.D., *Trapped in the Mirror: Adult Children of Narcissists in Their Struggle for Self* (New York: William Morrow, 1992), 180.

2. American Psychiatric Association, *Diagnostic and Statistical Manual of Mental Disorders*, 4th ed., text revision (Washington, D.C.: American Psychiatric Association, 2000), 717.

CHAPTER 2

1. Jan L. Waldron, *Giving Away Simone* (New York: Anchor, 1997).

2. *Terms of Endearment*, 1983 (movie).

3. *Pieces of April*, 2003 (movie).

4. *Postcards from the Edge*, 1990 (movie).

5. Nicole Stansbury, *Places to Look for a Mother* (New York: Carroll & Graf, 2002), 95–96.

CHAPTER 3

1. Rebecca Wells, *Divine Secrets of the Ya-Ya Sisterhood* (New York: HarperCollins, 1996), 251.

2. *Gypsy: A Musical Fable*, 1959 (musical, directed by Jerome Robbins); *Gypsy*, 1962 (movie).

3. *Mermaids*, 1990 (movie).

4. From poem "Dear Mommy" by Linda Vaughan, M.A., Denver, Colorado.

5. *Terms of Endearment*, 1983 (movie).

6. *Beaches*, 1988 (movie).

7. *The Other Sister*, 1999 (movie).

8. Rebecca Wells, *Divine Secrets of the Ya-Ya Sisterhood* (New York: Harper Collins, 1996), 60, 225.

9. Billie Holiday, from *Divine Secrets of the Ya-Ya Sisterhood* (New York: HarperCollins, 1996), 1.

10. Michael Wilmington, movie review: *The Mother*, June 17, 2004 (www.chicago.metromix.com/movies/review/movie-review-the-mother/158925/content).

CHAPTER 4

1. Stephanie Donaldson-Pressman and Robert Pressman, *The Narcissistic Family* (New York: Lexington Books, 1994), 18.

2. Salvador Minuchin, *Families and Family Therapy* (Cambridge: Harvard University Press, 1974).

CHAPTER 5

1. *Postcards from the Edge,* 1990 (movie).

2. Alexander Lowen, M.D., *Narcissism: Denial of the True Self* (New York: Touchstone, 1985), ix.

3. *USA Today*, "Generation Y's Goal? (Wealth and Fame)," January 10, 2007.

4. Harris Interactive, *The Supergirl Dilemma: Girls Grapple with the Mounting Pressure of Expectations* (New York: Girls Incorporated, 2006), 3. See also http://www.girlsinc.org/ic/page.php?id=2.4.30.

5. Ibid., 3.

6. Audrey D. Brashich, *All Made Up* (New York: Walker, 2006), 67–68.

7. *Only Two Percent of Women Describe Themselves as Beautiful*: article at www.dove.com/real_beauty/news.asp?id=566, 2004.

8. Information regarding brachioplasty surgery and cost from PlasticSurgeons.com.

9. *Allure* magazine, September 2006, 118.

10. Brashich, *All Made Up*, 65.

CHAPTER 6

1. According to Wikipedia, Mary Marvel is a comic book superheroine who first appeared in 1942. She is the twin sister of Captain Marvel's alter ego, Billy Batson. Mary and her brother Billy were orphans. When calling upon her special powers, she is transformed into an adult version of her late mother.

2. Stephanie Donaldson-Pressman and Robert Pressman, *The Narcissistic Family* (New York: Lexington Books, 1994), 133.

3. American Psychiatric Association, *Diagnostic and Statistical Manual of Mental Disorders*, 4th ed., text revision (Washington, D.C.: American Psychiatric Association, 2000), 717.

4. "Introduction of the Impostor Syndrome," online article at www.counseling.caltech.edu/articles/The%20Imposter%20Syndrome.htm.

5. Pauline Rose Clance and Suzanne Imes, "The Impostor Phenomenon in High-Achieving Women: Dynamics and Therapeutic Intervention," *Psychotherapy Theory, Research and Practice,* vol. 15, no. 3, fall 1978, 2.

6. Marianne Williamson, *A Return to Love: Reflections on the Principles of a Course in Miracles* (New York: HarperCollins, 1992), 190–91.

CHAPTER 7

1. Margaret Drabble, *The Peppered Moth* (Orlando, FL: Harcourt, 2001), 163.

CHAPTER 8

1. Eric Fromm, *The Art of Loving* (New York: Bantam, 1956), 50.

2. Rebecca Wells, *Divine Secrets of the Ya-Ya Sisterhood* (New York: HarperCollins, 1996), 393.

CHAPTER 10

1. *Postcards from the Edge*, 1990 (movie).

2. Elisabeth Kübler-Ross, *On Death and Dying* (New York: Macmillan, 1969).

CHAPTER 11

1. Elizabeth Strout, *Amy and Isabelle* (New York: Random House, 1999).

2. Murray Bowen, *Family Therapy in Clinical Practice* (New York: Jason Aronson, 1978), 539.

3. Ibid., 539–42.

4. Ann and Barry Ulanov, *Cinderella and Her Sisters: The Envied and the Envying* (Philadelphia: The Westminster Press, 1983), 19.

5. James F. Masterson, M.D., *The Search for the Real Self: Unmasking the Personality Disorders of Our Age* (New York: Free Press, 1990), 42–46.

CHAPTER 12

1. Agnes Repplier, *The Treasure Chest* (New York: HarperCollins, 1995).

2. The concepts of "the internal mother" and "the collapse" are illustrated creatively in Dr. Clarissa Pinkola Estes's spellbinding story collection on her CD *Warming the Stone Child* (Boulder, CO: Sounds True, Boulder, 1990).

3. American Psychiatric Association, *Diagnostic and Statistical Manual of Mental Disorders*, 4th ed., text revision (Washington, D.C.: American Psychiatric Association, 2000), 715.

4. Ibid., 468.

5. Thomas J. Leonard, *The Portable Coach* (New York: Scribner, 1998), 19.

6. Dr. James Gregory is a family practice physician at Gregory, Barnhart and Weingart, in Thornton, Colorado.

CHAPTER 13

1. Victoria Secunda, *When You and Your Mother Can't Be Friends: Resolving the Most Complicated Relationship of Your Life* (New York: Dell, 1990), xv.

2. Murray Bowen, *Family Therapy in Clinical Practice* (New York: Jason Aronson, 1978), 534.

3. These categories are defined by the Mountain States Employers Council, Inc., in the booklet *Generations: Working Together*, 6.

4. Lewis Smedes, *Shame and Grace: Healing the Shame We Don't Deserve* (San Francisco: HarperCollins, 1993).

5. Henry Nouwen, *The Only Necessary Thing* (New York: Crossroad, 1999).

CHAPTER 14

1. Alice Miller, online interview, 2006: www.alice-miller.com/interviews_en.php?page=2.

2. Elan Golomb, *Trapped in the Mirror: Adult Children of Narcissists in Their Struggle for Self* (New York: William Morrow, 1992), 199.

3. American Psychiatric Association, *Diagnostic and Statistical Manual of Mental Disorders*, 4th ed., text revision (Washington, D.C.: American Psychiatric Association, 2000), 717.

SUGGESTED READING AND
MOVIE VIEWING SOURCE LISTS

BOOKS

Adams, Alice. *Almost Perfect*. New York: Washington Square Press, 1993.

Agnew, Eleanor, and Robideaux, Sharon. *My Mama's Waltz*. New York: Pocket Books, 1998.

Apter, Terri. *You Don't Really Know Me: Why Mothers and Daughters Fight and How Both Can Win*. New York: Norton, 2004.

Bassoff, Evelyn. *Mothers and Daughters: Loving and Letting Go*. New York: New American Library, 1988.

Beattie, Melody. *Beyond Codependency: And Getting Better All the Time*. Center City, MN: Hazelden Foundation, 1989.

————. *Codependent No More: How to Stop Controlling Others and Start Caring for Yourself*. New York: Harper and Row, 1987.

Beren, Phyllis. *Narcissistic Disorders in Children and Adolescents*. Northvale, NJ: Jason Aronson, 1998.

Bowlby, John. *A Secure Base: Parent-Child Attachment and Healthy Human Development*. London: HarperCollins, 1988.

Boynton, Marilyn, and Dell, Mary. *Goodbye Mother Hello Woman: Reweaving the Daughter Mother Relationship*. Oakland, CA: New Harbinger, 1995.

Brashich, Audrey D. *All Made Up: A Girl's Guide to Seeing Through Celebrity Hype . . . and Celebrating Real Beauty*. New York: Walker, 2006.

Brenner, Helene G. *I Know I'm in There Somewhere: A Woman's Guide to Finding Her Inner Voice and Living a Life of Authenticity.* New York: Penguin, 2003.

Brown, Byron. *Soul Without Shame: A Guide to Liberating Yourself from the Judge Within.* Boston: Shambhala, 1999.

Brown, Nina W. *Loving the Self-Absorbed: How to Create a More Satisfying Relationship with a Narcissistic Partner.* Oakland, CA: New Harbinger, 2003.

———. *Children of the Self-Absorbed: A Grown-Up's Guide to Getting Over Narcissistic Parents.* Oakland, CA: New Harbinger, 2001.

Campbell, W. Keith. *When You Love a Man Who Loves Himself.* Naperville, IL: Sourcebooks, 2005.

Carter, Steven, and Sokol, Julia. *Help! I'm in Love with a Narcissist.* New York: M. Evans, 2005.

Chesler, Phyllis. *Woman's Inhumanity to Woman.* New York: Avalon, 2001.

Cloud, Townsend. *The Mom Factor.* Grand Rapids, MI: Zondervan, 1996.

Colman, Andrew M. *Oxford Dictionary of Psychology.* New York: Oxford University Press, 2001.

Corkille Briggs, Dorothy. *Celebrate Your Self: Making Life Work for You.* New York: Doubleday, 1977.

Cowan, Connell, and Kinder, Melvyn. *Smart Women, Foolish Choices: Finding the Right Men, Avoiding the Wrong Ones.* New York: Signet, 1985.

Debold, Elizabeth; Wilson, Marie; and Malavé, Idelisse. *Mother Daughter Revolution: From Good Girls to Great Women.* New York: Bantam, 1994.

Delinsky, Barbara. *For My Daughters.* New York: HarperCollins, 1994.

Donaldson-Pressman, Stephanie, and Pressman, Robert M. *The Narcissistic Family.* New York: Lexington Books, 1994.

Drabble, Margaret. *The Peppered Moth.* Orlando, FL: Harcourt, 2001.

Edelman, Hope. *Motherless Daughters.* New York: Addison-Wesley, 1995.

Elium, Don, and Elium, Jeanne. *Raising a Daughter: Parents and the Awakening of a Healthy Woman.* Berkeley, CA: Celestial Arts, 1994.

Ellis, Albert, and Harper, Robert. A. *A Guide to Rational Living.* Chatsworth, CA: Wilshire, 1974.

Fenchel, Gerd H. *The Mother-Daughter Relationship: Echoes Through Time.* Northvale, NJ: Jason Aronson, 1998.

Flook, Marie. *My Sister Life.* New York: Random House, 1998.

Forrest, Gary G. *Alcoholism, Narcissism and Psychopathology.* Northvale, NJ: Jason Aronson, 1994.

Forward, Susan. *Toxic Parents: Overcoming Their Hurtful Legacy and Reclaiming Your Life.* New York: Bantam, 1989.

Fox, Paula. *Borrowed Finery.* New York: Henry Holt, 1999.

Friday, Nancy. *My Mother, My Self: The Daughter's Search for Identity.* New York: Dell, 1977

Golomb, Elan. *Trapped in the Mirror: Adult Children of Narcissists in Their Struggle for Self.* New York: William Morrow, 1992.

Herst, Charney. *For Mothers of Difficult Daughters: How to Enrich and Repair the Bond in Adulthood.* New York: Random House, 1998.

Hirigoyen, Marie-France. *Stalking the Soul: Emotional Abuse and the Erosion of Identity.* New York: Helen Marx Books, 2000.

Hotchkiss, Sandy. *Why Is It Always About You? Saving Yourself from the Narcissists in Your Life.* New York: Simon & Schuster, 2002.

Judd, Wynonna. *Coming Home to Myself.* New York: Penguin, 2005.

Karen, Robert. *Becoming Attached: First Relationships and How They Shape Our Capacity to Love.* New York: Warner, 1994.

Kieves, Tama. *This Time I Dance! Trusting the Journey of Creating the Work You Love.* New York: Penguin, 2002.

Lachkar, Joan. *The Many Faces of Abuse: Treating the Emotional Abuse of High-Functioning Women.* Northvale, NJ: Jason Aronson, 1998.

———. *The Narcissistic/Borderline Couple: The Psychoanalytic Perspective on Marital Treatments.* Philadelphia, PA: Brunner/Mazel, 1992.

Lazarre, Jane. *The Mother Knot.* New York: Dell, 1976.

Lowen, Alexander. *Narcissism: Denial of the True Self.* New York: Touchstone, 1985.

Masterson, James F. *The Search for the Real Self: Unmasking the Personality Disorders of Our Age.* New York: Simon & Schuster, 1988.

Meadow, Phyllis W., and Spotnitz, Hyman. *Treatment of the Narcissistic Neurosis*. Northvale, NJ: Jason Aronson, 1995.

Michaels, Lynn. *Mother of the Bride*. New York: Ballantine, 2002.

Miller, Alice. *The Drama of the Gifted Child: The Search for the True Self*, 3rd ed. New York: HarperCollins, 1996.

Minuchin, Salvador. *Families and Family Therapy*. Cambridge, MA: Harvard University Press, 1974.

Morrison, Andrew P. *Essential Papers on Narcissism*. New York: New York University Press, 1986.

Northrup, Christiane. *Mother-Daughter Wisdom: Understanding the Crucial Link Between Mothers, Daughters and Health*. New York: Bantam Doubleday Dell, 2005.

Norwood, Robin. *Women Who Love Too Much: When You Keep Wishing and Hoping He'll Change*. New York: Simon & Schuster, 1985.

O'Neill, Eugene. *Long Day's Journey Into Night*. New Haven, CT: Yale University Press, 1956.

Peck, M. Scott. *People of the Lie: The Hope for Healing Human Evil*. New York: Simon & Schuster, 1983.

Pipher, Mary. *Reviving Ophelia: Saving the Selves of Adolescent Girls*. New York: Ballantine, 1994.

Richo, David. *How to Be an Adult in Relationships: The Five Keys to Mindful Loving*. Boston: Shambhala, 2002.

Robinson, Marilynne. *Housekeeping*. New York: Farrar, Straus and Giroux, 1980.

Schiraldi, Glenn R. *The Post-Traumatic Stress Disorder Source Book: A Guide to Healing, Recovery, and Growth*. New York: McGraw-Hill, 2000.

Secunda, Victoria. *When Madness Comes Home: Help and Hope for Children, Siblings, and Partners of the Mentally Ill*. New York: Hyperion, 1997.

————. *When You and Your Mother Can't Be Friends: Resolving the Most Complicated Relationship of Your Life*. New York: Dell, 1990.

Snyderman, Nancy, and Streep, Peg. *Girl in the Mirror: Mothers and Daughters in the Years of Adolescence*. New York: Hyperion, 2002.

Solomon, Marion F. *Narcissism and Intimacy: Love and Marriage in an Age of Confusion*. New York: W. W. Norton, 1992.

Sprinkle, Patricia H. *Women Who Do Too Much: How to Stop Doing It All and Start Enjoying Your Life*. Grand Rapids, MI: Zondervan, 1992.

Stansbury, Nicole. *Places to Look for a Mother*. New York: Carroll & Graf, 2002.

Stone, Hal, and Stone, Sidra. *Embracing Your Inner Critic*. New York: HarperCollins, 1993.

Ulanov, Ann and Barry. *Cinderella and Her Sisters: The Envied and the Envying*. Philadelphia: Westminster Press, 1983.

Viorst, Judith. *Necessary Losses: The Loves, Illusions, Dependencies, and Impossible Expectations That All of Us Have to Give Up in Order to Grow*. New York: Ballantine, 1986.

Wells, Rebecca. *Divine Secrets of the Ya-Ya Sisterhood*. New York: HarperCollins, 1996.

Wilde, Oscar. *The Picture of Dorian Gray*. New York: Barnes and Noble, 1995.

Williams, Tennessee. *The Glass Menagerie*. New York: Random House, 1945.

Williamson, Marianne. *A Woman's Worth*. New York: Random House, 1993.

Wurmser, Leon. *The Mask of Shame*. Northvale, NJ: Jason Aronson, 1995.

Yudofsky, Stuart C. *Fatal Flaws: Navigating Destructive Relationships with People with Disorders of Personality and Character*. Arlington, VA: American Psychiatric Publishing, 2005.

MOVIES, WITH DIRECTORS
(MOST ARE AVAILABLE ON VIDEOCASSETTE OR DVD.)

Baby Boom, 1987 (Charles Shyer)

Beaches, 1988 (Garry Marshall)

Because I Said So, 2007 (Michael Lehmann)

Divine Secrets of the Ya-Ya Sisterhood, 2002 (Callie Khouri)

Georgia Rule, 2007 (Garry Marshall)

Gia, 1998 (Michael Cristofer)

Gypsy, 1962 (Mervyn LeRoy)

Mermaids, 1990 (Richard Benjamin)

Miss Potter, 2006 (Chris Noonan)

Mommie Dearest, 1981 (Frank Perry)

Mona Lisa Smile, 2003 (Mike Newell)

Ordinary People, 1980 (Robert Redford)

Pieces of April, 2003 (Peter Hedges)

Postcards from the Edge, 1990 (Mike Nichols)

Prozac Nation, 2003 (Erik Skjoldbjaerg)

Something to Talk About, 1995 (Lasse Hallstrom)

Terms of Endearment, 1983 (James L. Brooks)

The Devil Wears Prada, 2006 (David Frankel)

The Mother, 2003 (Roger Michell)

The Other Sister, 1999 (Garry Marshall)

The Perfect Man, 2005 (Mark Rosman)

White Oleander, 2002 (Peter Kosminsky)

INDEX

ABOUT THE AUTHOR

Karyl McBride, Ph.D., LMFT, is a licensed marriage and family therapist in Denver, Colorado, with over 28 years in public and private practice. She specializes in treating clients with dysfunctional-family-of-origin issues. For the past 17 years, Dr. McBride has been involved in private research concerning children of narcissistic parents, with a primary focus on women raised by narcissistic mothers. She has treated many daughters of narcissistic mothers in her private practice.

Additional information on services provided and background experience can be found on Dr. McBride's private practice Web site at www.karylmcbridephd.com. The *Never Good Enough* book Web site, which includes a discussion forum for daughters of narcissistic mothers, can be found at www.nevergoodenough.com.

To contact Dr. McBride for speaking engagements, workshops, or further information, e-mail her at dr.mcbride @att.net.